How to Get
Along
with Black People

How to Get Along with Black People

A HANDBOOK FOR WHITE FOLKS*

And Some Black Folks Too

by Sheila Rush
and Chris Clark

Foreword by Bill Cosby

THE THIRD PRESS

JOSEPH OKPAKU PUBLISHING COMPANY, INC.

444 CENTRAL PARK WEST, NEW YORK, N.Y. 10025

TP-8

To my parents
SHEILA RUSH

To Mommy and the men in my life
CHRIS CLARK

Contents

How to Get
Along
with Black People

Foreword

This book will aid a whole lot of people so that they will no longer be uptight about name-calling when it is time to call names.

For instance, let us say you had found an employee who was not doing the job but were afraid to fire him because he was black. Now, in all honesty, you know that he is not doing the "gig" (job) but you kept him on for twenty years because you were afraid of the NAACP, SNCC, CORE, RANK, ZAPP, and the Italian Anti-defamation League, all of which he has promised he would call down on you if he was ever fired.

After reading this handbook you will be able to look this dude dead in the face and say to him, "Blood, I am afraid to say that the time between you and me is beginning to sway. Your appointments have been strangled and as much as I tried to angle the true feelings of my own racism, and upon looking into the prism of life, I can say but to you, 'Nigger, you're fired.' "

Now, you can turn the same thing around and say to a white friend you were afraid to fire, "Honkie, you are fired."

*

Whitecat at a bar looking at four black cats in the same gray suits. He is sitting there.

It is a black conversation. They are rapping and slapping hands. He is sitting by himself and he loves "Negroes" and he feels he would like to belong. (A great deal of this is paranoia; "Are they talking about me?")

So he conquers his fear and goes over to the guys and it is always one of two conversations.

Conversation Number One: He slaps one cat on the shoulder keeping a smile on his face and says, half high: "Listen, I have a story and I think you guys will appreciate this one."

He then tells a story about black people which may or may not be in good taste. Either way it turns them off. So some of the black guys wonder:

a. where he got the story
b. what nerves he has to come barging in without regard for courtesy or concern as to whether or not the black people would appreciate it.

Besides, his story is really one about white people as told by some white Uncle Remus.

Or not wanting to belong, Whitecat tries

Conversation Number Two: (with a smile and a slap on the back)

"Gee whiz, I wish to hell I knew what you guys were talking about. I have been sitting over there for a half hour trying to understand what you were saying. What do you mean, James Brown is "bad"? I thought most black people like James Brown."

The black cats stare at him in utter wonderment. They say absolutely nothing to him. The white cat doesn't know how to handle this. He proves his blackness by calling a chick whom no one would touch, a beautiful woman.

*

First of all, most bourgeois people are full of sh--. We —and I include myself—have our values, our materialistic values which I feel are full of cr--, according to the way we use the twelve cars, two houses, a wife, three old ladies, six hookers, and our children in private, semi-private and downright lonely schools.

We are basically full of this thing because we have to act out our roles not only as persons who own all of these things, but also we have to act like we really know how to handle all of them.

If we want to go sailing, we have a sailboat, and we have to know how to sail. So we buy the complete sailboat uniform, take lessons and then we set out to sail. Land-ho! and the boom swings around and hits you on the forehead . . . Bonk! . . . and knocks you in the water, you and your brand new sail suit, and all.

Now there are all sorts of problems in trying to enjoy what you've earned in addition to getting bumped into the water. We sometimes find ourselves in contact with something that we have never before had to deal with, economically or socially. We cannot get away from them. Running up our a– as fast as they can run is the black man.

He can readily be seen breathing hard, running perhaps

twice as fast (but, thank God, managing to stay behind us, which is very difficult to do). He talks like us, he knows our "language." He knows about our mothers, our fathers, our sexual habits, the kind of food we eat, and the special wines that we enjoy. Red, white, and some other color.

And he seems to be a pretty nice guy. At the office when we speak to him, it's straight business. He is right with me and I am right with him. And I discuss this with my wife, and she says, "Well, if he's not like all the others we've seen on TV, on the news, why not invite him over for dinner."

We invite him to dinner. He brings a beautiful——uh, er, color'd er Negr,,, er (this is after the revolution) BLACK woman who is dressed in some African clothes with huge, long, gold earrings. And her hair is the same length as his. Afro style. Yep.

We invite them in and I introduce my wife, who looks very white to me now, I tell them "I dig" and my wife says she's "hip" but somehow, between the pre-dinner cocktails and sitting at the table, they leave. For the life of me, I cannot figure out why.

He said that I was full of sh--, and he left. I heard the car engine start up, my wife and I were in the kitchen holding the silver platter full of pigs' feet, chitterlings, and something from the jaws of the hog with which we had practiced eating without throwing up, I said to her, "Throw that sh-- in the garbage. I don't know what I said but they left. I'll take you to McDonald's."

Months later this dude reads about himself here. He rushes to his neighborhood bookstore and buys a carload of *How to Get Along with Black People* or he gets two copies in the mail for Christmas——one from his black friends and one from——guess who? his wife who is still smarting from having wasted her practice on chitterlings. Mr. Whitecat is much happier after reading this book. In fact, he feels so very comfortable that he puts three copies on his own Christmas list. One to his boss (underlining *A Handbook for White Folks*), one to his bourgeois black friend (underlining *And Some Black Folks Too*), and a special copy to the President, underlining everything!

BILL COSBY

October, 1971

Introduction

The racial fury of the sixties has ended. Overtly, at least. But no one would say "The Problem" is solved; it has always been an American thorn, though it need not be.

Of course, there will always be those whites whose fear of the black presence will cause them to panic and sell their homes at a loss, commute three hours each day from suburb to city and back, or place their children in private schools they can't afford.

But there are other whites who comprehend the futility of "solving" problems by avoiding them. Although for years racial conflicts have been blamed on black people, lately, a new awareness is developing and many whites are beginning to suspect that considerable responsibility for racial difficulties is theirs.

Many of them who hoped to find help in the seemingly endless number of black books, articles, studies and reports were disappointed. While gaining some insight into problems, they found no assistance as to what they might *do* to preclude the possibility of tension in their personal dealing with black people.

Few problems defy solution. It's simply a matter of pinpointing the difficulties, analyzing the causes, and carefully thinking through the remedies. Still, some might argue that handbooks are too simplistic a way of dealing with complicated personal matters, that certain problems are insoluble. To them we say: "Nothing is, but thinking makes it so."

Handbooks have helped people in bed. And not just to get to sleep. We anticipate that our book will be followed by similar handbooks on how to get along with, say, Italians, Jews, or perhaps Laplanders or Serbians. Who can tell?

Why, then, do the goodwill attempts between the races rarely come off? Because whites, even those with the best of intentions, find it difficult to shake off their past racial indoctrination—whitewashing, if you will. Years of childhood training in the wrong direction are not countered by post-adolescent awareness. Whites need to know the numerous little *faux pas* that cause discomfort and worse— and the ways in which they can be relieved.

Racial differences need not have existed, but since they do, the authors hope this handbook will be helpful to the thousands of people like those whose private and confidential inquiries have prompted them to publish it. Ultimately this book will make it easier for whites to get along with blacks.

What's in it for black people? Obviously, we could all do with decreased irritation.

1

Eeny-Meeny-Miny-Mo (or What to Call "Them")

Eeny-Meeny-Miny-Mo
Catch a ——— by the toe
If he hollers, let him go
Eeny-Meeny-Miny-Mo

White people find themselves blithely starting this children's rhyme, and then, midway through the second line, running into the inevitable point where the word for what-you-catch-by-the-toe is "nigger." Whether or not to use this traditional term becomes a problem if someone black is present. If so, the white reacts with surprise at how sneakily the word popped up and awkwardness about what to quickly substitute for it.

Coffee-breaks, company luncheons and private parties and dinners create similar dilemmas for whites over what to call "these people." For years, "colored" led the list of preferred "pseudonyms"; it was sufficiently general to make the group so designated feel just *slightly* different. You know, "people" like anybody else, but with a little dash of color. Later, "Negro" with its important capital N was an attempt to dignify a people degraded and diminished in its sense of self. "Afro-American," more recent, implies something assertive but consistent with the practice of hyphenating Americans, like Italian-Americans and Polish-Americans. The term "black," downright insulting not too long ago, has gained popularity since blacks have realized that they were not going to be white. So a term placing blacks in stark contrast to whites was needed. Black. That's "versus" white.

Deciding which of the labels to use these days is not always easy, and a wrong choice can cause abrupt shifts in potentially friendly winds. Different blacks prefer different labels.

Race labels have always had a "for colored only" use. Whites seldom refer to their own race or color, except to describe racial encounters. One never reads that the President appointed Mr. Big Shot, "a white," to a Cabinet position. Still, even though whites started this business of categorizing by color, the *changes* in the terms designating that separateness are black creations. Which label a given black prefers depends mainly upon how he views blacks and whites. Age, birthplace, skin color and education are helpful clues for detecting what such attitudes are.

Some Clues

Age

Age is a useful guide. There is a rule of thumb: the older the black person, the greater the benefit of the doubt he's likely to give the white.

Among older blacks, two groups stand out. One believes that the racial situation is unlikely to change and that it would behoove blacks to accommodate to it. The other strongly believes that in the long run "right will out," and that there will indeed be justice for all. Note the passive posture in each attitude: things will or will not change—there is little sense of one's own ability to change things.

The younger generation, while skeptical of whites, is less likely to accommodate. Many of them, having benefited from the hard work of their parents, have more alternatives and consequently are assertive in the face of white attitudes. More savvy, whether well educated or not; whites cannot "put them on." Gift horses are indeed looked in the mouth, not to mention other anatomical parts. Thus where whites expect gratitude, young blacks feel that anything whites do "for the blacks" is designed to save a white system. And an essential past part of that system has been to put and *keep* blacks down.

Despite these apparent differences, there is not much of a generation gap among blacks. Both older and younger ones have recognized that things were racially wrong; the differences between them lie in their reactions to those wrongs. Many older blacks have felt the razor edge of discrimination; they are often those with the most scars and concomitant bitterness, though suppressed. Alert young blacks are aware of this and respect these veterans of the racial wars. Ralph Ellison, in his *Invisible Man*, made this point:

> I am not ashamed of my grandparents for having been slaves. I am only ashamed of myself for having at one time been ashamed. About eighty-five years ago, they were told that they were free, united with others of our country in everything pertaining to the common good, and, in everything social, separate like the fingers of the hand. And they believed it. They exulted in it. They stayed in their place, worked hard, and brought up my father to do the same. But my grandfather . . . was an odd guy. . . . It was he who caused the trouble. On his deathbed, he called my father to him and said, "Son, after I'm gone I want you to keep up the good fight. I never told you, but our life is a war and I have been a traitor all my born days, a spy in the enemy's country ever since I give up my gun back in the Reconstruction. Live with your head in the lion's mouth. I want you to overcome 'em with yeses, undermine 'em with grins, agree 'em to death and destruction, let 'em swoller you till they vomit or bust wide open." They thought the old man had gone out of his mind. He had been the meekest of men. The younger children were rushed from the room, the shades drawn and the flame of the lamp turned so low that it sputtered on the wick like the old man's breathing. "Learn it to the younguns," he whispered fiercely; then he died.

Of course, there is the problem of whites being unable to discern age among blacks. Fat can make a young woman look and move like an old one; bad health also ages people. The extensive use of dentures, a result of poverty and poor nutrition, can also age a person. On the other hand, the tendency of dark skin not to wrinkle can give the impression of greater youth.

BIRTHPLACE

The area of the country where a person has spent his formative years is another factor contributing to his racial outlook. Southern blacks related the "better" position of their Northern cousins to rumors about improved relations with whites "up north." Distance made for dreams.

Claude Brown in his moving reflections on northward migration in *Manchild in the Promised Land* has written:

> These were the poorest people of the South, who poured into New York City during the decade following the Great Depression. These migrants were told that unlimited opportunities for prosperity existed in New York and that there was no "color problem" there. They were told that Negroes lived in houses with bathrooms, electricity, running water, and indoor toilets. To them, this was the "promised land" that Mammy had been singing about in the cotton fields for many years.

Only recently, since the waves of northern riots and urban joblessness, have southern blacks questioned this thinking. Southern blacks have lived with whites on clearer and closer terms, and have learned better how to handle them; they tend to be less impatient, more ingratiating, and ultimately more manipulative of whites. Beneath it all, they know basically how whites really feel about blacks, have a keener appreciation for relative power and of their own ability over the long run to alter the status quo.

Whitney Young, Floyd McKissick, and Martin Luther King, Jr., are men who have dealt effectively with whites and they are all from the South. Their tactics reveal a fundamental understanding not only of relative power positions but, equally important, white psychology. Although different types of leaders, the novelty and distinction of their approaches have left indelible marks on black thinking and American history.

Because official and overt oppression was less openly practised in the north, it was harder for blacks to develop a keen sense of their position in relation to whites. They lived in a nebulous in-between where the distance between what was preached and what was practiced could not readily be measured. Northern blacks from non-ghetto, integrated areas may be more sanguine and relaxed about whites, especially if they were treated as "special" by them.

Malcolm X, on the other hand, grew up in a Michigan ghetto and witnessed what many southern blacks experienced: the lynching of his father by a white mob. His mother, left a widow, knew degradation Northern-style: welfare. She eventually went insane.

Stokeley Carmichael and Roy Innis both came from the Caribbean, where slavery ended earlier than did the American version. There blacks developed clearer ideas of power from having seen black majorities and blacks in control of businesses, schools and governments. Their British ties arm them with an arrogance towards Americans which makes them less likely to concede much to white people. As one old Jamaican was heard to say in clipped, Caribbean accent, "I don't dislike *all* white people. I think some of them are just as good as I am."

Skin Color

This is a tricky clue. Fair-skinned Negroes, resembling whites and therefore more acceptable to them, had it better in past years. They were regarded as "easy on the eyes," as though blackness caused visual pain. As the products of black and white sexual contact they were "looked after" by their white sires, allowed to be closer to the master ("house niggers") and frequently favored by their black mothers. They often took advantage of such privileges and flaunted them before the darker "field niggers." In later years, the lighter ones developed an internal apartheid system, excluding their darker brethren from parties, fraternities and sororities, professional schools and marriage.

Many of the fairest ones, leaving the slave stigma behind forever, "passed" for white. Rarely would their darker brothers betray their secret; passing was seen as practical, a part of surviving.

There are *two* divisions of fair-skinned Negroes, one more common than the other. The first group includes those whose whole families were "light" (as blacks say), who enjoyed deriving the special benefits of their separateness from darker, "low-life" blacks, and were cut short of those special goodies after the racial events of the 1960's made tokenisms and the role these "light-skinned" Negroes played in them suspect. Before that time the *one* black employee in a non-menial position with white companies was often light-skinned. (How slavery days do hold on!)

The other, much less common group among such lighter Negroes had darker beloved relatives (the range of color tones within a single black family can be considerable) and even in pre-1960 days *disliked* being mistaken for white and took no racial advantage of their fairer skin, in the sense of lording it over their darker relatives. To the extent they had it easier than their darker siblings, for example in getting jobs, it was treated as a joke on whites, who could be so stupid as to care how much "white blood" a given Negro had. They knew that children of the same parents obviously had the same "blood" though their skin tones differed.

These light-skinned blacks are now often more vociferously hostile to whites than the blackest of blacks. Although they have rejected the easy out of passing or accepting special treatment, darker blacks for historical reasons still find them suspect.

EDUCATION

In the past, education was used by blacks to differentiate themselves from other blacks. A college education, regardless of where obtained, was usually a guarantee of entry into white-oriented elite black groups. Many also saw it as capable of "transforming" them into near-whites, the glorious, much sought after metamorphosis. Among older, often southern blacks, there is an effortful clipping of words that smacks of their idea of sounding white and therefore well-educated.

Now, however, well educated blacks, especially younger ones, appreciate what they regard as the survival mechanisms of uneducated blacks. These are the humor, the mother-wit (wisdom), the conscious putting-down of "Whitey" without his knowing it (otherwise it was the lynching rope), and a way with expressions. A well-known remark by Joe Louis is a good example:

Everyone knew Joe wasn't smart by the usual measure and came from a poor, uneducated family. Yet his expressions were truly wise in that they got to the nub of things. Before one of his fights, it was said that Billy Conn, the white contender, was fast-moving in the ring, which might give him the edge over Louis. Joe's response, in basic black, was "He can run, but he can't hide."

In the same vein, Muhammad Ali's summary comment, "No Vietnamese ever called me nigger" does the same thing. Just a pithy phrase to indicate a developed position and philosophy as to why he would not be inducted into the United States armed forces.

Even educated blacks knew the ungrammatical dialect and could lapse into it at will. They would reserve it for all-black gatherings and talk "correctly" around whites and other strangers. In a sense, they were truly bilingual. Younger blacks, sometimes out of a slightly defensive attitude about not being from the ghetto, are using the comfortable dialect almost to the exclusion of ordinary grammatical speech. In the need to establish and keep ghetto credentials, they use language as a leveler and unifying force.

Education is now less used by blacks to scale the ladder of "whiteness." If anything, more and more blacks educated at white prestige institutions are resisting white lures and discovering an identity of interest with lower-income blacks. They are aware that whites have often used class distinctions among blacks to divide black people and to destroy the potential for unity.

The Integration Index

The various factors presented add up to people. Age, birthplace, skin color, and education largely determine black attitudes towards whites. The following portraits, an "Integration Index," will introduce whites to a range of black types and assist in the task of deciding which label to use and when.

READY RICHARD

To begin. He is over 40, has attended college, grew up believing that if he acted "proper" (that's a black term to mean correct-in-white-terms), didn't offend by being boisterous or too assertive (that's something like racial militancy) and showed he accepted all American values, he would be treated like any man (read *white* man).

Ready Richards mostly smile in the presence of whites and cast constantly assessing eyes at other blacks to see how they measure up on the whites' acceptance scale. They are displeased if these other blacks rank either too high or too low on that scale. The reason is that Ready Richard believes that whites are willing to include only a few Negroes within their various spheres. And Richard wants it to be him; thus he competes with other blacks for white attention, approval and favors.

This species is so called because he is most ready to accept all things white, except the kind of overt discrimination which would exclude himself and those like him. He is sometimes called Tom.

He is found with whites when he can manage it. He

mostly manages it. He prefers "Negro" but will answer to "colored." He tends to be lighter-skinned.

He is at the top of the Integration Index in that he is a 100-percenter. He opposes any form of black separation, voluntary or otherwise, except, perhaps, at the family Thanksgiving Dinner.

There is, fortunately, a little-known side to Ready Richard. It was mainly his need to survive which produced his careful behavior towards whites. With the racial assertion of the sixties, a long-suppressed part of him surfaced. He was finally able to acknowledge the offenses and slights he too had experienced in the company of his much sought-after white associates; he was forced to connect his experiences with those of other blacks. Although he has not forsaken his usual circles, he has become slightly more assertive, but only slightly. He still, however, refuses to acknowledge the debt he owes the "rowdy," "low-life" blacks who made the new climate possible.

HUSTLIN' SAM

This guy is a product of the civil rights events of the sixties.

He is an ideological chameleon.

Like a trained Irish setter, he can scent subtle shifts in the militancy tolerance of white Americans and accommodates himself accordingly. He holds himself out as an intermediary between misunderstood, oppressed blacks and unenlightened, primarily liberal whites. He can be found either in prestige consulting firms, having parlayed a one-time militant stand into lucrative contracts, or roaming through the grass roots, which he uses as platforms for his political ambitions. He looks mainly to whites for his sense of status and importance. Some Sams wear Brooks Brothers suits; others, colorful danshikis and affect Africanisms.

If his base is permanently grass-rooted, he frequently journeys out to foreign territory for cocktail parties, benefits and other hob-nobbings. To keep whites interested he may employ a threatening demeanor. Whites either like him or adopt him.

The Sams cover the color spectrum, though if they are dark, tend to be tall and what whites regard as good-looking; they can be anywhere from 25 to 50. They are usually northern, glib, charming, and shrewd assessors of the extent to which whites can be harangued, pushed or challenged.

Unlike Ready Richard, the hundred percenter, Hustlin' Sam checks in at 75% on the Integration Index, for he feels blacks have some good things going for them, like him. Richard, if given a chance, would become white. Furthermore, Sam is quite aware that his success and legitimacy among whites depend upon black support or contact.

Sam insists upon being referred to as "black" but wouldn't quibble about the size of the "b." (See below.)

KWAME JONES

Mr. Kwame Jones typifies a new breed. He frequently draws from the best of traditionally white resources—especially education—yet remains quite skeptical about where it will get him. He is open to being wooed by white Americans, but not to being won. His sense of history is yet too vivid for that.

Basically, Mister Jones is keenly aware that whites are responsible for the worst conditions of black life and feels no inferiority or shame about what that means. What he's called is up to you, but he prefers "black" or "Afro-American." He may work in an all-black neighborhood, but he could be found in an all-white corporation.

He is not awed by white institutions for he sees their mistakes and realizes that resources like money and media-control make whites less vulnerable to exposure. He understands power.

Kwame Jones is so named because he looks to primarily black sources for a substantial part of his identification. (Kwame is an African first name.) Jones, of course, is the flat and common all-American stamp that could apply to any person, as for example, Bobby Jones.

Mr. Jones realizes that his parents got caught short relying totally on the American dream. He is not un-American, in J. Edgar Hoover's sense of the word, though he has been treated that way. He considers it ironic that the major, most long-termed official in the United States government focuses not on the un-American treatment of blacks but on their potential for an un-American response.

Mr. Jones is young, college-educated and comes in various shades. He is at the 50% level on the Integration Index. The speed of future changes in the status of blacks in the concrete terms of education, housing and jobs will determine his movement on the Index.

It is he who is the nation's question-mark. He can go either way.

Ghetto Jim

The black whom whites know best—and least—is Ghetto Jim. On the one hand he has worked among them for years, as a messenger, servant, or day laborer—those positions traditionally "reserved" for blacks. On the other hand, there has been practically no social contact between Jim and whites, who see him as fearsome and threatening.

He takes no white rules seriously: they hold no usefulness or real application to his ghettoized life. He speaks another language, is the great initiator of what whites have come to know as slang or "hip" expressions and lives with the level of danger that rats, junkies, malnutrition, hostile teachers and crooked cops pose.

Jim embarrasses Ready Richard with his ungrammatical, rowdy style. Sam romanticizes him out of a need to justify his dependence upon the likes of Jim. Kwame sees him clearly as a human being with foibles, faults, and strengths, but, more importantly, as a greater victim of oppression because he lacks the objectivity and insight necessary for transcending the black predicament. Although the Jims generally are a-political, of late he can be found at the lower echelons of some anti-poverty organizations.

He is a major influence. His clothing, with its colors and weird blends of patterns (considered tasteless before) is now seen on Madison Avenue. His mystery and *apparently* indestructible ability to cope are the subject of numerous inquiries, artistic and academic.

For him, white people are square and without "style." He also regards them as corrupt; his contacts with whites confirm it.

He cares least about white customs as a model for his behavior; they have been irrelevant to his life except insofar as they have tried to put him down. In that sense, he is at or around the 5% point on the Integration Index.

In one other respect, though, he is at the 100% point. That has to do with money. He likes his money integrated

—it can be any color: green or white. White people are useful insofar as they aid this objective. The same goes for
blacks.

He is perennially young, usually dark-skinned, and
doesn't care what you call him so long as it isn't "nigger."

A LAST PORTRAIT

What you have read does not pretend to be an exhaustive
or "scientific" treatment of the infinite range of black types
and racial responses.

Women, for example, are not separately sketched mainly
because male and female types often coincide. The main
exception to this is, of course, the domestic, who usually
measures high on the Integration Index, mainly because
most of her waking day is spent in a milieu more affluent
than her own. She comes to appreciate the ease, material
comfort and the seeming graciousness of a life-style that she
attributes to whiteness. She's not a full hundred percenter,
however, because though a regular witness to debutante
parties with champagne and foie gras, she has also been
privy to questionable morality and shady business practices.
It is she, as Dick Gregory put it, who washes your dirty un-
derwear. Many whites have relied upon her—the one black
with whom they have had continuing and frequently intimate contact—for racial guidance and insights, a role
which many domestics have dutifully assumed as part of
the job. Realize, however, that in her mind, the employment has required that she tell the white employer what he
wanted to hear. She was therefore likely to suggest that
riots were unwarranted, that many blacks were rowdy and
uncouth and that in general blacks were satisfied. Whites

who relied exclusively upon this source of racial wisdom still find themselves in need of guidance.

Which Label for Whom?

What black people want to be called has varied with the dominant mood of a particular era. Therefore, the term in vogue at the time when any particular black was growing up frequently is *the* term that person will prefer—barring other experiences that keep him abreast with the thinking of younger blacks. (These days, untold numbers of black middle-class parents are forcing themselves to use "black" in the presence of their Afro-coiffed offspring who ruthlessly scrutinize them for "Uncle-Tomism," congenital or acquired.)

After Emancipation, as the "freeing" of the slaves has been called, "colored" was the most respectful form of address. It was popular in the days when the melting-pot theory was in vogue, but before it was pointed out who wasn't exactly melting.

Blacks who still prefer "colored" are normally white-oriented and assess their worth in proportion to the amount of their manifest white blood. They tend to be much older, normally hark from the south and are aghast at the more challenging attitudes of the young generation of blacks.

"Negro" is preferred by a group which is far more elusive and difficult to define, partly because it includes a substantial number of persons who sometimes refer to themselves as blacks but frequently lapse back into "Negro" from habit and from the sheer exertion of having to remember to say "black" for relatively long periods of time. "Negroes" are generally over 30 and in occupations or professions which have required some adjustment to the changing attitudes of younger blacks: teachers, for example. Civil servants, isolated by their sense of employment security from more oppressed blacks and convinced that passing a government test makes them intellectually superior, often prefer "Negro." Then there are those who were "firsts" (you know, the first to integrate this or that) and also that handful who are reluctant to offend those whites still unadjusted to hearing "black" uttered by blacks.

"Afro-American" is a current, widely acceptable label. It pleases proud types who stress the "Afro" part; it just slightly jars the ear of the Ready Richards or standard black middle-streamers, but they tolerate the term because they can identify with the last half of the phrase, the "American" part. The utility of "Afro-American" to whites is greatest when it is difficult to discern the kind of black being addressed, but may startle whites who have ignored that blacks have a motherland.

"Black" (with a small b) should be used with all those under 30 and with anyone who looks whites straight in the eye when speaking. It is also welcome to those who wear the natural "Afro" hairstyle.

"Black" (with the large B) is more appropriate when addressing nationalists, those favoring residential, educational and political separation from whites. In conversation, the use of the large B is indicated by pronouncing "black" slightly more emphatically and with a brief pause after the word.

On Using "Nigger"

The increased and less guarded social contact between blacks and whites, and the openness with which blacks and whites now discuss racial problems has resulted in well-meaning whites using the term "nigger" *not* to offend but to casually illustrate sometimes valid points. "Nigger" originated as a term of derision and abuse for enslaved blacks. It was subsequently adopted by blacks and put to the double use of expressing derision or affection for another black, depending upon the context. Even among blacks, though, the derogatory use of "nigger" can result in bodily injury. It is important that whites who have recently taken to using this term in the presence of blacks, whose goodwill they assume or seek, understand how such usage enrages the average black, even when the term is used to exemplify what the white person deems an objectionable practice. Such usage is akin to a child, prohibited from using profanity, reading aloud from the profane passages of the biblical Songs of Solomon.

There is, however, one group of whites whose use of the term "nigger" by way of illustration, produces a lesser reaction. He is the liberal white southerner. Like the black, he is accustomed to the more regular and easy use of the term. He is not self-conscious with, nor newly discovering it. He can legitimately mimic the real racists from his part of the country in their use of it. His intonation of the word, being southern, is familiar to the black ear. (Northern accents give the expression an especially harsh ring.) The "converted" white southerner seems more direct, more honest than the Northern white liberal and therefore relatively less suspect. Nevertheless, the longtime derisive use of "nigger" by whites has rendered most blacks deaf to the tonal differences in usage. Consequently, an absolute ban seems the only solution.

Blacks can refer to themselves and call one another "nigger" and it is quite all right. As with family and romantic pet names, it is intimate and affectionate but inappropriate for someone not so connected to use the term. The story is told that a white man in court complained to the black judge that the black defendant had called him a mother-fucker. The black judge informed the white complainant that in the black community "M-F" can be a term of endearment and admiration. And it often is. But the white man's reaction shows that whites take offense if called "M-F". Thus, a white calling a black an "M-F" had best watch out. Them's fighting words.

It is no guide to whites to call blacks what blacks call themselves.

To Sum Up

As for how you refer to black people, terms should not be used indiscriminately. You now have a range of possibilities and are acquainted with the "types" most likely to prefer "colored" to "Afro-American." But when in doubt, it is a toss-up between "black" (with a small b) and "Afro-American."

The white reader now knows that skin shade, age and birthplace influence how blacks look at whites. It is probable that the younger, darker, northern black is less likely to assume your racial goodwill.

You now have an Integration Index which is a ready reference for recognizing common black "types." Because inherently limited, it should not be treated as definitive or exhaustive. It does give you in its character portraits a sense of the interplay of the various factors shaping black attitudes towards whites.

2

Hob-Nobbing

The nice thing about most social situations is that planning is possible, unlike those innumerable other occasions which "just happen." With a little advance thought, hosts can avoid the tensions and irritations sometimes stemming from interracial contact. Guest list made, champagne ordered, bartender hired, canapes ready, the hostess anticipates the pleasant exchanges and gossipy tid-bits her guests will share. There may be a little hitch, a slight flutter of apprehension when she speculates about how things will go—since blacks too are invited. Will it be all right? Will everyone be comfortable? What can she do to make it work?

Cocktails and Parties

Cocktail parties are often large, impersonal affairs in that they are work-related, given to honor a distinguished per-

son, or to lighten a series of seminars, lectures or
conferences. Accordingly, blacks are showing up more frequently at these occasions than at others which are based
on greater intimacy.

Some cultural differences come into play here and make
these events a bit trying for blacks. For them, parties have
meant fun, frivolity, and casual conversation with friends
and acquaintances. The social event as an extension of
business, politics or work is essentially a white phenomenon. Apart from the fact that the collecting and culti-
vating of "contacts" has not only been less necessary
because of the job pursuits blacks were limited to, blacks
generally regard social gatherings among their own as times
of relaxation and release.

Even with the more intimate and leisurely parties at
white homes, blacks find many of the same practices which
characterize cocktail parties. Here again, white people seem
to come together more for personal and professional ad-
vancement than for the sheer enjoyment of seeing and
being with people they like—or might like—in a relaxed
setting. Increasing numbers of blacks invited to such social
events report what has long been rumored among blacks—
that whites do not usually dance at their parties, even those
which last past midnight.

For whites interested not only in making the party more
comfortable and enjoyable for blacks but perhaps for themselves, a glimpse at how dancing and conversation function
at black parties might be instructive.

First of all, there's the talk. Blacks even have an expression for it; they say, "Talk that talk," a banter which blacks
later called "rapping"—until that expression got commer-
cialized. The conversation consists of jokes, teasing, and

affectionate near-insults, called "signifying". Though sometimes quite personal, these remarks which might seem
negative or critical to the outsider are taken good-naturedly.
It is understood that there is no malice and that the comments are to provide a release and an outlet for deeper feelings which would seem overly sentimental or embarrassing
if expressed directly.

The dynamics of dancing at the black party are even
more revealing. Any mention of dancing raises in the white
mind the obvious superior dancing ability of blacks. Nor-
man Podhoretz described his middle-aged white reaction to
this phenomenon quite movingly.

> "I have come to value physical grace very highly, and I
> am now capable of aching with all my being when I
> notice a Negro couple on the dance floor. . . . They are
> on the kinds of terms with their own bodies that I should
> like to be on with mine, and for that precious quality they
> seem blessed to me."
>
> (*Commentary*—Feb. '63)
> "My Negro Problem—And Ours"

Dancing in part helps to satisfy that curiosity we feel
about the other person. It is a chance to hold hands, to
touch, and to move together in an enjoyable unison. For
blacks, it makes talk unnecessary. One complaint blacks
have made about white parties is that whites frequently
want to talk while dancing, thereby interrupting the ab-
sorption and involvement in the physical movement.

Admittedly, these are difficult differences to resolve. One
approach is to lighten the conversation, unless the shop-talk
redounds ultimately to the economic benefit of the particular black. (See below Dinners: Subjects and Conversations

to Avoid.) Although younger whites are learning to dance rather adequately by black standards, older whites still have trouble; their efforts to "get with it" through dancing are sometimes too exaggerated or forced to be fun. If the dancing is too much of a strain and does not come naturally, an occasional "soul" record would help immeasurably.

OTHER PROBLEMS

The problem of how to get a handful of black guests circulating freely at a party is one that many whites, with all their social experience, find sticky. Many hostesses will introduce a black guest to a white one and then quickly disappear, praying that no special attention to the black guest will be necessary. Other well-intentioned Perle Mestas will maneuver black guests in the direction of other black guests, in defiance of the old saying that opposites attract. Once at a large New York party, an extremely gracious white hostess, seconds after greeting a young black woman at the door, escorted her to a young African woman who was alone and sipping her drink. The hostess was visibly relieved at the arrival of the only person who she felt could mitigate the social isolation of this woman.

Now, from the black point of view, what was wrong here? Well, the first thing is that the hostess thrust the two people together solely on the basis of color. It is similar to swiftly introducing two octagenarians at a party attended mainly by young people. Unlike the sharing of alma maters or scientific specialties, race, like age, is not a neutral "interest." Of course, blacks frequently seek out other blacks at social gatherings. But the important distinction is that they do it on their own; they dislike having it forced upon them. It is too reminiscent of segregation.

When the black guest or speaker at a gathering is a prominent person, whites on occasion have found it extremely difficult to resist sharing the eminence of such a great man with all who might benefit from his aura. It has happened, consequently, that house servants, faithful and true hotel employees, and other blacks who serve whites have been summoned forth on such occasions to shake hands and exchange greetings with the famous guest. For all the democratically inclined, let it be noted that there is nothing objectionable or racially offensive about such a practice *per se*. What is objectionable is its exclusive application to situations where the prominent guest is black. In the interest of consistency and in an attempt to achieve the long espoused American ideal of obliterating social distinctions, we urge simply that all prominent *white* guests or speakers also be introduced to the kitchen help—black or white.

Dinners

Fried chicken anyone? Most whites have advanced beyond thinking that the ideal menu for a black dinner guest is fried chicken and watermelon, but there are difficulties peculiar to dinners which flow from the more intimate setting, the greater time spent together, and the inability to leave if things get close.

Nothing tries the patience, good will, and social restraint of blacks invited to dinner by whites more than spending most of the evening discussing racial problems. Racial problems are to blacks as mortgage difficulties, marital strife, and the requirements of success in these highly competitive United States are to whites: they are a fact of life, ever-present, difficult, and preferably avoided. Yet, while whites would rarely inquire—however politely—about their friends' mortgage payments ("How much do you owe on your house, John?"), marital disagreements ("Tell me Steve, do you and your wife curse when you argue?") or efforts to gain approval in a dog-eat-dog job situation ("Now isn't it true, Don, that you laugh at the boss' jokes in order to get the promotion?"), they regularly ask the opinions of black social guests about the countless aspects of American racial strife, as though blacks alone were the sole actors in this continuing American drama.

At a recent dinner party, shortly after being introduced to a young black couple in the arts, a young businessman recently appointed to the board of trustees at his college, was waiting patiently for the black woman to wind up her remarks on the state of the American theater. At last, there was a pause in the conversation. He said to the young woman, "Here's something that may interest you." And she (suspecting what it was about):

"Yes, what is it?"

"I understand that you're a trustee at your alma mater. So am I! I was elected about a year ago. At the last meeting we had a very difficult matter to resolve."

She braced for the inevitable. The young man continued, with obvious relish.

"You see," he continued, "an alumna bequeathed a fund to Dennison for scholarships but specified that the support go only to white students. The board had to decide whether or not to accept the bequest, and the discussion about it was heated. Turns out, they rejected it by one vote. You might say I made the difference." Smiling, he continued, "How would your board have decided this?"

Resolved to end the discussion, she said firmly, "I really don't know." She then turned to a young, white woman listening to all this, whose smile the black woman interpreted as understanding. They began happily discussing the problems of working mothers.

Around blacks, whites suffer a temporary amnesia with respect to topics they normally discuss. It is as though their interest in opera, theater, world politics, the stock market, their companies, their children, etc., etc., evaporates with the appearance of blacks, whom they sidle up to, quite amicably, to ask or express an opinion about black-white conflict, or black-black conflict, most recently.

Other blacks, not quite so adroit as our young woman, find themselves—for the duration of an evening—plied with a seemingly endless stream of racial questions. They go away race-weary, exhausted, and often angry at still another tedious encounter, vowing to think twice before accepting the next invitation.

Dinners with friends should be light, happy affairs—a refuge from the problems of day-to-day life rather than a verbal telescoping of life's ever-present and unavoidable trials. It sometimes happens, of course, that blacks themselves will introduce racial subjects. In such instances, the purpose is sometimes to assess the situation or to discuss what they feel knowledgeable about and know will interest whites. Whites can help by confining discussions of race to those far more numerous occasions when they are in the exclusive company of whites. By the time the black guests' turn comes, hopefully the whites also will be race-weary.

Second only to being expected to discuss racial problems is the distaste most blacks experience when being queried about "what they do" by whites at social situations. On the one hand, such questions are understandable, given the American correlation of social status with occupation or profession. However, even in these days of increasingly visible black achievements, there are still the noticeable "oohs" and "ahs" when whites learn that blacks are something other than singers, dancers, or basketball players. If the job of the black person advances the interests of black people, the white person tenaciously interrogates the black person about the manifold details of his efforts. Even the black in his own business or profession, normally private matters, is not spared this relentless questioning. It is as though the activities of blacks were in the public domain and they would be obliged to open their ledger books if only they had remembered to bring them along to the party. Now there is nothing wrong with this kind of exchange of information in and of itself, provided it *is* an exchange. The trouble is that usually what should be a two-way street turns into a dead-end—for blacks. For when blacks venture to question their white interrogators about their activities (what are your company's hiring policies? expansion plans? will there be a public offering? how do you get your contracts?), they draw either a blank or a quick "Oh let's not discuss something so boring! What you're doing is sooooo much more interesting . . ."

The advice? End the one-way traffic.

GET ANOTHER ONE
It is characteristic of all human beings to project their frustrations and concerns onto others, to see in others what

they refuse to recognize in themselves. Accordingly, many whites assume that their black dinner guests will be ill at ease in the sole company of whites, and frequently will invite a second set of blacks. Less conscious is another reason: the white hosts see the presence of the second black couple as removing some of the pressure on them to pay special attention to one couple; the second couple frees them to attend to their other guests.

Since the first-invited black guests are the paramount concern of the host and hostess, they give little thought to the second couple and generally no consideration to compatibility of interest, background or social level between the two black couples. More often than not, the effect of this well-intentioned though haphazard mixing is that the black guests, after a few perfunctory remarks, will say very little to each other and spend the evening largely avoiding each others' eyes while chit-chatting with the whites. The evening will probably be strained and boring unless the black guests discover mutual friends and interests; then, more likely than not, they will spend most of the evening talking to each other and before leaving, make elaborate plans to see one another again.

Commendably, the white hosts here are trying to avoid tokenism. But in "getting another one," they are really using the second couple impersonally. And that's offensive.

Dating and Marriage

Interracial dating and marriage has always been a touchy, explosive issue for blacks and whites. For years, the main opposition came primarily from whites, with blacks mainly neutral or favorably disposed. Lately, as white resistance has lessened, black opposition has increased. The vicissitudes of these relationships have always been subject to the prevailing racial climate.

SOME BACKGROUND

The era of anti-miscegenation laws, lynching of black men for actual or fantasied rapes of white women, and the passing of fair-skinned blacks across racial lines is well-documented. (Even today, many white women think that every black man is out to rape her, while on the subway, in a bus, or on the street.) Too little has been said, however, about the extensive sexual contact between the white man and black women, during slavery and afterwards. His interest in such illicit relationships is not much discussed among whites but is common knowledge among blacks, who normally have a white male ancestor or two and whose fair-skin, light eyes, or less kinky hair attest to some past "mixing." In slavery of course, blacks had no legal right to marry anyone, black or white, so the legitimizing of an interracial liaison was out of the question. Afterwards, the same situation prevailed since no white, regardless of how many black children he fathered, was prepared to jeopardize his status, name, or position by marrying a black woman or acknowledging their children. Power being what it was during such times, force was often involved in such relationships, but it must be said that the black female may sometimes have willingly submitted since it meant greater material advantages and a lighter and consequently favored child. Nor should one completely rule out the possibility of genuine affection. Many white fathers of illegitimate black children did make "arrangements" for the care and education of these offspring. An educated black "elite" thus got its start.

Despite this far more common white-initiated contact with black women, only relationships between black men and white women provoked strong opprobrium from whites. Where lynching was not a real threat or possibility, opposition took the form of social ostracization and abuse of the white woman who violated The Code. Because she frequently lost her own friends and relatives, she looked to the black community for friendships, where she was usually quite welcome. Her children of course were regarded as black and in some circles, after a time, she too became regarded as practically black in the sense that no restraint about racial remarks, jokes, or comments was exercised in her presence. The one notable exception to this open-door policy was the small but growing number of black female elite, who took pride in their white ancestry and whose attractiveness to prosperous black men was largely because of their white features. For them, the availability of white women to black men was threatening.

Today, things are different. There are fewer extreme sanctions when black men date or marry white women, and the practice is rather widespread. However, there is a growing black opposition to such relationships; they are seen as undermining the growing self-esteem and cohesiveness of blacks as a people. The argument runs thus: for too long, blacks have seen whites as a standard of beauty and acceptability; absolute prohibition is necessary in order to eradicate the negative cultural influences of whites; in the past, black women have been the main casualty of interracial dating and marriage in the sense that their kind of beauty—fuller features, darker skin, kinky hair—was different from the media image and therefore less desirable. Black women also argue: when the black man was being messed over by your white man, when he was down, we cared for him. Now that he is black and proud, you want him. Still others maintain that the white woman among blacks is a "Fifth Column"— a spy for the "enemy."

What kinds of black men appear to move towards white women? In the past, there were the intellectual and artistic types who believed there were few black female counterparts who could share their interests. The intellectual or artistic black woman is a fairly recent phenomenon, the black poet Phyllis Wheatley notwithstanding. The average college-educated black woman was forced to be fairly security-minded and less willing to risk starving with some black painter, writer, or artist who was likely not to "make it." Many politically radical blacks for the same reasons, chose white women. Also, because black women themselves were not unaffected by white standards of beauty, they rejected the more Negroid, dark, or African man who found white women more receptive. Then there is a handful of blacks, reared in mainly white circumstances, who never learned that certain essence of blackness, best described— to the extent that it's possible—as "soul." Many of these guys also date or marry white. Then there are those individual blacks who fall in love with specific whites.

The myth of dark flesh still prevails. This causes a lot of black women to shun and reject overtures from white men. The assumption of both races is that these men are interested in black women for "all the wrong reasons," usually not including marriage. Most "self-respecting," middle-class types of black women have protected themselves from

any suggestion of impropriety by ruling out these relationships altogether. These women are frequently the ones
most vociferously opposed to black men dating white
women, for they have consciously chosen not to exercise
their interracial option and the marital market being what
it is, want black men to do likewise. Among these black
women, the myth of dark flesh prevails.

Still, there is a pronounced minority trend in that certain
black women are choosing to marry white men. The most
obvious group are entertainers who have "made it." A long
list comes to mind: Lena Horne, Pearl Bailey, Eartha Kitt,
Dorothy Dandridge, Diahann Carroll, Nina Simone, Leslie
Uggams, Roberta Flack, Diana Ross. In selecting white
partners, they seem to be looking mainly for a man who
can "fit" into their cabaret-society life-style. Many of the
men they marry, on the other hand, have no particular distinction and work as managers or agents for their illustrious
spouses.

When one moves beyond entertainment circles to the
black female educated at white colleges and universities,
especially the more "exclusive" ones, power seems to be an
important factor in the search for a white spouse. Most
women, white or black have known that marriage is the
perfect vehicle for partaking of wealth, prestige, position,
and achievement, which in America are most likely at-
tained by white men. (Women's Lib notwithstanding).
Ironically, these black women now marry white men for
precisely the same reason that not too long ago whites
would not marry them. By such marriages, they now move
into a world from which black men are still, for the most
part, excluded.

SOME PROBLEMS

Once we thought we were different, not black or white,
something unique, special. Why couldn't everyone be like
us? There'd be no race or any other problems. Arrogance
and blind stupidity. We were two racists living together,
knowing only the myth of each other, speaking a language
of homonyms. From such different places with different
ways, we offended and didn't know we did and by the time
it was over, the myth had become reality.

from *Blues Child Baby*

Relationships are difficult. Everybody knows that. But
the black-white relationship, where each is American, is
beset not only with the common difficulties and the racial
pressures from outside but also by the racial attitudes and
expectation the partners bring to each other.

There are some whites who repeatedly remind the black
partner of what he or she is sacrificing for this particular relationship. Most partners—of any color—would expect to
be informed when friends, relatives, or jobs are lost. But
here, the question is one of degree. What the average black
objects to is the martyr syndrome—constant reminders of
what has been given up for interracial love. Especially since
the black partner has sacrificed at least as much as his or
her white spouse.

And then, there is the white female who is over-protective
towards the black partner. Women, reared as they are, have
been prepared for the caring and tending role. Some white
women gravitate towards black men whom they see as need-
ing more soothing and support in their state of oppression
than the average American white male. What could be a
virtue, however, often becomes a vice. Very often, she al-

lows the black male to become excessively dependent upon her not only emotionally but economically. *Blueschild Baby* describes this succinctly.

> Shouldn't've been no big thing, had been stealing and taking from her regular, though she said nothing and pretended it didn't happen. Rather than force a confrontation, she'd leave more money for me to take. So guilty, she indulged and tried to understand my every weakness, making me weaker and more dependent. Hated her understanding and insistence on thinking she understood. That all we had to do was talk about it, communicate and somehow it'd all work out. She couldn't understand how things and incidents unrelated to us in any way should have such profound effects on our relationship. She loved me and my attitude changed with the fortunes of my people in the pages of the *Times*.

> We were wrong. She knew but wouldn't let go, trying to suck me of all strength. So weak and near drowned, hooked and in need of money, I couldn't leave. Complying with my degradation I stayed and sunk deeper.

Many of these problems reflect what may be sado-masochistic tendencies in the participants. Such a phenomenon is decidedly present in what might be called the "Getting Even" Syndrome and both the white and the black might be doing this. In marrying or dating white, this black is thumbing his nose at one of the major prohibitions white society imposes upon him. He is saying if I can't have it all, then at least I'll have one of the things you cherish most: your women. He sometimes carries this need to get even into the inter-action with the white partner and in countless subtle ways makes the partner "pay" for all white wrongs. This often means public embarrassment for the white partner or frequent angry diatribes about the pervasiveness of racism.

From the white standpoint, getting even means mainly scandalizing parents. In one fell swoop, they retaliate for all parental brutalities, actual or imagined. With tongue in cheek, the white writer of the following letter anticipates the effect on her parents of her "decision" to marry a black:

Dear Mother and Dad,

I know I've been at college four months now, and I apologize for not having contacted you sooner, but many things have happened to me since I last saw you.

The first thing is that there was a fire in my dormitory and in getting out of the burning building, I had to jump out of a window. When I landed on the ground, I discovered I had broken my ankle.

The fellow from the gas station came rushing over to help me and in as much as I had no place to live, he invited me over to live in his apartment, so I have been living with him for the last three months.

Don't be concerned; I am pregnant but knowing your liberal points of view, I'm sure you won't object to his color. We figure it'll be a beautiful baby, a blend of black and white.

Well, anyhow, when our plans are clearer I'll let you know. I feel fine.

Your loving daughter,
Jane

P.S. Now that you have come to terms with the above, you can disregard all of it. What's really happened is that I flunked psychology.

By contrast, that may not be so bad, huh? (Excuse the joke.)

Both races sometimes use interracial relationships as a way of avoiding deep involvement. For many people, commitment is deliberately curtailed during stages of life, such as college, when exploration is paramount. Then there are other instances where circumscription of involvement seems chronic; people who are avoiding marriage will regularly date interracially as a protection. The built-in obstacles in these relationships are easy excuses when excuses are needed.

Flag-waving in these relationships is not unknown. Particularly during the civil rights era of the sixties, interracial unions appeared to be chosen as extensions of political principles. The couples saw themselves as living embodiments of the highest democratic ideals. It was: "See America, this is what equality is all about." Now what's wrong with this? Such flag-wavers are hung up on the intellectual and rational externals that have little to do with the subtle and not-so-subtle nuances and sharings that deepen a relationship.

Showing off is another matter. Some whites and blacks are known to do it. Blacks sometimes use whites for display purposes; for the male, the attractive white woman is seen as increasing his prestige in the eyes of both black and white men. For the women having a partner of the opposite race makes people notice them. They stand out. Therefore their racial choice may indicate a bid for attention. For the sexually insecure white male, the black woman is publicly squired about as clear and convincing proof of virility. A more obvious form of showing off is en-

gaged in by the partner with a photographic memory who
regularly recounts with relish every racial slight visited upon
the brave young couple.

Some Hints

Many interracial relationships fare rather poorly in America for the reasons mentioned. Tact, sensitivity and understanding are essential but not always enough to protect
these couples from the hostility and antagonism of relatives, friends, and especially strangers white *and* black.
There are two groups of interracial couples which seem to
weather these trials better than others: those where one
partner is not American. The foreign-born partner, whether
white or black, seems relatively independent of conventional American racial responses; this seems to help. The
second group which fares better are those later-wed who are
older, wiser, and experienced enough to care less about public opinion. Many of these relationships are a last grasp at
happiness, now that family ties and similar conventional
pressures have become irrelevant.

Hints? This area is a thicket; or you might call it a can of
worms. Although the best armor may be self-awareness and
clarity about motives, the following pointers will also be
helpful.

Discuss racial problems or incidents openly and candidly
but avoid agonizing over them. A sense of humor helps.

Whites should exercise restraint in seeking to "find out
about blacks." While the black partner might appreciate
an interest in food or music preferences, zealous researching
into the folk ways of blacks is resented.

White women in particular should be careful not to
dispute, contradict, or challenge the black partner *publicly*.

They just don't like it, especially coming from a white woman.

Very few blacks, male or female, enjoy public displays of affection.

For onlookers, a simple adage: live and let live.

Doormen

Doormen are traditionally a New York phenomenon (though spreading to other cities). The average doorman sees himself as having a job to do—the protection of the tenants in the building from uninvited or unwanted strangers. To him, black people are both. Even best dressed blacks have problems, but sloppy whites get through. In the absence of clear and precise instructions from the white tenants, their black guests are normally required to produce unassailable credentials before the zealous sentry will let them pass.

It would seem that the best solution would be for whites interested in more than a one-shot visit from their black friends to inform their doormen that black guests are expected and that they are to be treated politely. Whether or not the names of the guests should also be given to the doorman is questionable. One group of blacks, possibly a minority, enjoys what seems to be the personal attention from the doorman who has been alerted to their coming and addresses them by name. "Good evening, Mr. and Mrs. George Washington Carver, Jr., the Van Slights are expecting you." Obviously, the hosts alerted the doorman to the color, arrival time, name, height and shoe size of the guests. Another group of blacks, perhaps more savvy and accustomed to the doorman bit, resents being made aware that they need special protection from the sentiments of this more or less inconsequential employee. They do not like the doorman telling them the apartment number and floor the moment their black faces come into view.

The white reader is probably thinking, "How do I know when to do what?" Although most of the shocking crimes in this country are committed by whites against each other, the need for protection against criminal intrusion focuses disproportionally on blacks. Thus the insult to the black guest. Without throwing caution to the winds, the management and tenants of such buildings can give their employees a simple set of instructions by which to screen *all* comers, black or white. Also the host or hostess should insist on equally polite treatment to all callers, black or white. The presumption against blacks is thereby eliminated.

Jokes

With the current sensitivity between blacks and whites, there are occasions when a racial joke will seem quite funny to a white person until he notices his black friend isn't laughing. To guffaw and then notice the black scowl can doom the budding black-white friendship.

In the past, the depiction of blacks in abused or demeaning situations was guaranteed to evoke laughter. Whites laughed at the shuffling, head scratching ways of Steppin' Fetchit (the name implies that he was to step and fetch it, presumably for his white master) and the servile Rochester with his rolling eyes and ingratiating manner. Both were shown as fearing ghosts (white shadows), often scared, slow, subservient, and most important, lacking even a shred of dignity.

In practically all humor, someone is made to look silly or slightly foolish. The test for whites in determining whether to laugh at a racial joke is whether the point of the joke is some universally valid insight about life or limited only to blacks. If the latter, chances are that blacks won't find it funny. Often blacks in such situations are apt to come back with a similar joke but with a white person at the butt of it. More often than not, the "open-minded" white joker who started it does not appreciate the black person's rejoinder.

In general, it is better for whites not to *tell* racial jokes. Light-skinned blacks, mistaken for white, report that such jokes told in "all-white" company serve only as put-downs. But whites might now ask, "Don't blacks tell racial jokes?" Yes, but generally the racial jokes blacks tell and laugh at show a black just barely escaping a white attempt to box him in. But even if whites were able to tell the very jokes blacks tell, there would still be problems.

Blacks making humor about blacks is similar to members of a family pointing out foibles, weaknesses or other deficiencies to other family members; the same criticism from someone outside the family would hardly be taken in the same way. Since blacks see few whites abounding in race-lessness, most white humor about blacks has a racial edge in it.

This basic affection for blacks is what makes Flip Wilson's Geraldine different from "Amos 'n' Andy." Geraldine is very much in control of her mostly white environment. As blacks would say, "She deals." With frolicking good humor, she lets whites presume nothing about her, her good will, or any romantic interest in them. And if she feels

her intimidating presence is not enough, she quickly in-
vokes the name of "Killer," her strong black man in the
background.

Amos 'n' Andy, on the other hand, showed blacks,
stumbling over attempts to use big words, with a penchant
for cheating friends with futile schemes of high finance and
success, and tyrannized by a black woman. With each program, it was a matter of what jam they would get themselves into this time. They were shown as helpless, amusing
children playing at being adults.

Spontaneous, open reactions to humanly funny incidents
are another matter entirely. Even if race is involved, it is
secondary. A young white salesman in a huge men's store
one day, after absent-mindedly giving away free samples of
sun tan lotion to all who passed, noticed with a start that a
very dark black man had refused a sample. The salesman
laughed. His comment was: "Man, I had to be kidding."

He was laughing at his own inattentiveness to a key detail. Race here was incidental.

Small Talk

"He's just the *nicest* person."
". . . just as qualified as anybody else."
"He would make it no matter what his color was."
"My maid calls me by my first name."
"One of my closest friends when I was a child was a little
colored girl."
"I almost dated that guy."
"——————————— (current Negro leader) really
makes a lot of sense."

Many whites, unaccustomed to black company, draw upon a surprisingly limited number of stock phrases. They apparently do not realize that such comments are dead give-a-ways of their social discomfort.

They recur so often since their purpose is to reassure blacks—or themselves—that they are racially OK. The effect of such hoisting of flags is tedious and burdensome for blacks, who have heard them so often and who could do with less talk and more action.

TRYIN' TO TALK BLACK

Black slang has long been the richest contribution to English as spoken by Americans. Although for years, whites of good taste regarded black slang as evidence of the inferior sensibilities of blacks, lately, all manner of white Americans—from the President to Madison Avenue copy writers, are adopting such black vernacular expressions as "soul-brother," "man," "right-on," "dig," "getting it together," "tell it like it is," and "doing your own thing." To be sure, blacks do not object to whites using such expressions among themselves; black slang not only infuses ordinary English with variety and interest, but the very use of the terms represent a breaking away from the uninspired pragmatism of American life. What blacks object to, however, are whites who mistakenly believe that by sprinkling their conversation with such 'hip' sounding words, they will gain the approval of blacks. Indeed, such a purpose reveals a total misunderstanding of the nature and function of such expressions in the lives of blacks.

Black argot is a form of speech evolved by a people unusually sensitive to the rhythm, tone, and musicality of speech—undoubtedly a carry-over from the African past.

The expressions derive their syntax and grammar from the black vernacular, which makes it particularly difficult for whites to adopt the expressions with the requisite ease. Thus, while one "tells it like it is," no black person ever "told it like it was." And while black folks may be "gettin' it together" only white folks (or cigarettes) "got it together." That is, the past tense makes it no longer a legitimately black phrase since blacks don't use certain expressions in the past tense.

The use of black slang in the forced, self-conscious, erroneous way that whites use it grates the black ear. Blacks are put off by the attempt. Once in a green moon a white person who has lived among blacks all his life comes along; he fully empathizes with the expressions and tradition which produced the vernacular and uses the expressions so naturally that it is hard to believe he is white. Young hippie-type whites also come close to doing the same thing. (See Schools.) The advice here: in matters of language, do your *own* thing.

3

Social Situations
(the Less Personal Ones)

Those social situations which "just happen" tend to catch people unawares. They are less intimate, imply no special relationship between the participants, and affect that majority of blacks who have no close white friends. They run the gamut from shopping and dining out to board meetings of the local United Fund appeal. The potential for irritation and abrasiveness is greater because of the relative anonymity of the people involved, who know that their contact will be brief. The racial difficulties arise because in many instances whites would prefer that the contact be even briefer.

White folks are frequently eliciting negative responses in these encounters without understanding what's ticking blacks off. Blacks pick up that whites are thinking certain things about them which trigger a summary treatment. What are these thoughts? They are the pre-conceptions which cause the whites to miss who a given black is or might be. They flow from fear, sometimes guilt. Whichever, blacks are the boogey-men. But the preconceptions have patterns, revealing certain themes or presumptions.

In these less personal situations, the understanding and foresight in the following illustrations should be helpful. The advice, in the final section, will be handy to whites in spotting their presumptions and changing the themes.

Shopping

The reader might think of department stores and small shops as rather neutral settings. For whites alone, perhaps they can be. Introduce the black element, however, and presumptions spring forth. One, which has some basis in fact, is that most blacks are poor. What black people object to is the next illogical leap that a black shopper is not a serious one and beyond that, a shoplifter.

If the white salesclerk suspects that the black is a shoplifter, he will rush up to him the moment he enters the store, stalk him through the racks, into the dressing room where, at carefully timed intervals, he will pull back the curtains to make sure the merchandise is still there. Poor timing, however, frequently embarrasses both shopper and clerk. When the salesperson is convinced that the black shopper is not a thief, he promptly disappears, leaving the black shopper to his own devices, (but perhaps whites have this problem too). Because it is a general practice to attribute the increase in crime wave to blacks only, there is a growing practice these days for small shops and especially haberdasheries, located in mixed neighborhoods to fasten their doors from the inside since this affords the salesclerks a chance to screen those who enter their stores—differentiating between the ever good-intentioned white shoppers and blacks who are always muggers and hold-up crooks.

Still another breed of white salesclerks are those self-appointed missionaries who seek to save blacks from their own pecuniary improvidence. Despite the clear labeling of prices in most stores, such clerks regularly—often apologetically—remind the black shopper of the cost of the item in which he has expressed interest, as though in addition to being poor, blacks are also illiterate.

A far more obvious attempt to "put down" the black shopper is to show him only the most expensive merchandise. The white watches for the squirm and the probable pretense on the part of the black that he can afford it but just doesn't "want that right now." All participants in this game know their roles too well.

Dining Out

Although blacks attest to some recent improvement in their treatment when eating out, specific annoyances linger. The primary tensions flow from the white waiter's attitude about serving blacks. This seems to be a particularly trying situation for whites in that they are called upon to wait upon blacks, a complete reversal of traditional roles.

Other dining problems for blacks concern seating and service. They find they have preferred rights to tables nearest the kitchen or, in the winter, closest to the cold drafts at the front door. And if there are serving stations scattered around the dining room, they note that maitre d's would have them as close as possible to the condiments, ice water, and serving trays. Apart from out and out racism, what's happening here is that restaurateurs assume that dining out is an infrequent event in the lives of blacks and consequently feel it a waste of time to court their future patronage.

Taxicabs

Many a white taxi-driver seems to have black on the brain. Despite this fixation, these cabbies—particularly in New York City—have managed regularly to pass up the potential black rider. (With the recent pressure of economics, however, there has been a diminution in selectivity of clientele—they are picking up blacks.)

After the momentous occasion of risking life and limb to chauffeur said passenger, the cabbie in an effort to be friendly, begins talking about topics of general interest like the weather and the cost of living. If the black passenger responds with comments, the cabbie—more often than not —quickly shifts into the second-gear of discussing rising crime, welfare costs, and "law and order" (the new code words for "Nigger"?).

A cabbie should expect silence, overt hostility, or worse if he broaches such subjects with the black passenger.

In one instance, when a young, black working girl was pointedly asked by the cabbie why she didn't go on welfare, she quickly retorted, "I will if you will." When the cabbie persisted with a sarcastic monologue on the virtues of her accepting the public dole, the young lady, as she was leaving the cab, failed to pay. As the shocked cab driver demanded the fare, she disappeared into the crowd, hollering that she had just that moment gone on welfare.

Policemen

Cops are "repeated offenders" when it comes to black citizens.

They have a difficult job, in that it requires them to get into more situations which can go wrong even if handled right. The possession of deadly weapons is that tipping factor which can so easily make the wrongs permanent.

Policemen, like doormen, spring to attention when a black face appears in a white setting. Whether changing a tire, apartment hunting or just driving through, the black in whiteland finds himself the center of criminal attention.

Behind police reactions is the conviction that blacks are not a part of the public they protect. They see themselves as guardians of whites—against blacks. Blacks know this and, like the policemen, are on guard. Thus, when there is any contact between the two, each comes with tension and the situation is set.

Blacks are not opposed to law and order. What blacks resent is the choice of laws cops choose to be concerned with. Call it selective enforcement.

A black 16-year-old might swipe a pocketbook and get three years while the cop who accepts the weekly payoff in the Harlem candystore and beats that same 16-year-old into insensibility "in the line of duty" is the guardian of law and order.

(Not to mention the white white-collar worker who embezzles thousands of dollars and is placed on probation.)

But blacks know better. Not one of the typical rackets—
narcotics, numbers, prostitution—could flourish without
police complicity. The dumbest of blacks knows that
today's technology of crime detection is too reliable for
such extensive crimes to continue rampantly. How much
respect for law can there be when a community's daily diet
includes such corruption?

Thus, there are two views of law and order. One white,
one black. Blacks ask only for consistency.

Those singing "law and order" most loudly would find a
chorus of supporters and a bunch of black recruits if they
were to adopt a single standard for all folks, policemen included.

Domestics

The democratic creed makes the master–servant relationship an awkward one in America. Even to call it that makes
some liberal-type employers wince. Thus, there is an effort
to deny the class and control differences by making the
black domestic "one of the family." That phrase is inappropriate for a couple of reasons. It connotes permanence, but
most domestics don't want to do such work forever. And it
points up in ironic fashion the white illusions about the relationship, for the first thing that enters the maid's mind
are those numerous occasions when she was treated quite
differently from the family!

THE PROBLEMS AS SHE SEES THEM
The major complaints of black domestics focus not so
much on the necessary aspects of the work; it is, after all,

cleaning up. There are, of course, the low-level grumblings about exactly how sloppy certain people can be; these amount to no more than the gripes anyone has about his or her work.

The focus here is on those aspects of contact with the employer which are not an inherent feature of the tasks of doing the cleaning, but which imply the special suitability of blacks for such work. A typical offense is the inferior quality of food offered the black domestic despite the abundance of better kinds in the larder. That is insulting; the very affluence of the employer makes it so. Such culinary distinctions reveal the employer's belief that the black recipient may not know the difference (the ignorance-theme), that such treatment is merited by virtue of some "special" classification (the inferiority-theme), that any such treatment can in no way matter to the recipient or that if it does matter she is sufficiently powerless to do anything about it. All of these "reasons" obviously explain the nature of the insult. Recall Portnoy in his "Complaint" detailing his mother's garbage leavings for the lunch of the "schwartze" who did their weekly cleaning.

Another valid complaint is the ever-so-nicey-nice suggestion that just-some-other-little-bittey duty be added, without extra compensation. Job descriptions, normal for white collar jobs, are non-existent for domestics. Thus, the very verbal or unspoken nature of the agreement between employer and employee may make for a kind of shifting definition of what is to be done. The problem is that additions are made, whereas substractions from duties are rare. Any person on the short end of this stick would object. Include black domestics.

Finally, the white employer thinks that exposing the

black domestic to his way of life, despite the hard work, is in itself a benefit, a gift, a nice extra. One middle-aged black lady had the occasion to accompany a white family to California, caring for the two children. Disneyland was to be a high point. Given the round-the-clock presence required, the level of energy required for a three year old and a six year old, the sight-seeing trips, eating out, and hotel duty at night, she was exhausted upon returning East. When she raised the need for time off, the lady of the house said, "Why? Didn't you have a good time?"

The "Slavery" Theme

Why is this a racial problem? Apart from the fact that an overwhelming disproportion of black females are forced into this kind of work, there is a presumption that the black female has no work alternatives, unlike white ones who can move in and out of clerical jobs, waitressing, and sales positions. This absence of options creates a near-slave tone to the work relationship as well as indifference and insensitivity to the amount of work the weaker sex can manage. The appellation of "girl", applied to black domestics as old as 80, has the same effect.

Campaigning and Politics

Despite the increasing use of television and newspapers to publicize candidates' platforms, many politicians make one or two incursions into black communities before election day. The mere fact that a politician ventures forth to talk to black people, however, doesn't mean that he isn't scrutinized for racial insensitivity. Few, however, have been quite so blatant as Spiro T. Agnew, who after a light once-over of a black enclave, announced, "When you've seen one ghetto, you've seen them all." Presumably, since Agnew took his unique perceptions to countless middle-American white communities, he must have there discovered an infinite variety which has escaped the most astute sociologists. While ghettoes were alike, suburbs were not?

BRAWN VS BRAINS: "THE STUPIDITY THEME"

Agnew aside, other politicians unwittingly reveal their Agnew-potential. They view black communities as foreign territories. As though in need of physical protection, the candidate projecting a liberal image normally chooses some well-known black person to accompany him on his political journeys. A look at the black escort is revealing. Robert F. Kennedy was accompanied by Rafer Johnson and Rosie Grier. Rockefeller chose Jackie Robinson. Nixon picked Lionel Hampton. Lindsay had Sugar Ray Robinson. These athletes and entertainers were hardly political strategists. They were black, had well-known names and faces, and were acceptable to audiences of both races—for different reasons. Around blacks the politician uses the athlete-entertainer to suggest to black audiences that he is their friend; this symbolism distracts attention from the failure to deliver on previous promises. In the white communities, the black companions enhance the "regular guy" image of the white politician; everybody loves an athlete (and of course, Lionel Hampton, Duke Ellington, Satchmo Armstrong, Count Basie and their likes are musical institutions by now).

No one would expect Joe Namath, invited along on a

political campaign, to be included in midnight political strategy sessions; but men of his color are. To the extent that blacks are consulted at all, it is informally, infrequently and without pay. And only on those few occasions where the white strategists spot a race issue.

RACE AIN'T JUST "RACIAL"

What these politicians don't know is that race lurks as a pivotal factor in practically every problem of national scope. Look at the cities. No society in history has survived the disintegration of its cities, but the real obstacle to creative and lasting solutions to America's urban decay are the racial feelings prompting the white exodus. Many of these white politicians overlook the fact that white paranoia about race has rent the social fabric. Consider the hold which Southern Congressman and Senators, elected solely on the basis of their racial sentiments, have on the United States legislature. An antiquated seniority system has vested power in this militaristic, parochial bunch of racists. Thus, no fresh forward-looking perspective is possible on broad issues such as peace, pollution, and space budgets.

WALKING THE RACIAL FENCE

Then there is the "Rights and Responsibilities" speech. Curiously, the white politician rarely uses this stock statement in addressing all-black audiences. Its special setting is the integrated gathering. Its purpose is to reassure the whites that any promises made to the blacks carry a price. Thus, when past achievement or proposed changes in laws to benefit blacks are announced, the politician quickly adds that with these rights go responsibilities. The politician sees the restoration of full human and civil rights to blacks as a gift, and he presumes the other whites feel the same. The emphasis on black responsibility as the price for any "rights" is a concession to the white view that blacks are always asking something, demanding everything of the government. What they've forgotten is that black blood, sweat, and tears—all free—built this nation. Blacks haven't forgotten.

WHAT EVERY POLITICIAN SHOULD KNOW: (white) The Harlems of the United States are becoming quite sophisticated about the distinctions between proposing legislation and vigorously pushing it. And voting records on a racially hot issue mean little unless the campaigner touting his record led a fight-to-the-death battle. What is clear is that the guaranteed annual income and rent subsidies never have the priority or the commitment of the SST issue, Supreme Court appointments, or the Gulf of Tonkin resolution. If these white politicians wish to continue to respond to race as a national priority only 'round riot time, they should hold to their present myopic course.

But no one is being fooled, least of all black folks. As one old Harlem resident muttered while walking away from the quadrennial appearance of Nelson Rockefeller, "Propose? What's a 'propose'? I could propose that whites turn black. But what would happen?"

Civic Contacts

Ever noticed that your Rotary Club, Boy Scouts troops, support-your-community theatre or help-your-local-orchestra groups, and charity or health campaigns don't attract many black volunteers? Any? Well, first of all, these efforts are usually neighborhood-based. And we all know who lives where. Next, volunteerism means giving either time or money, both of which are in short supply among blacks. Why is time so scarce? Much volunteer work is done by white women, whose husbands earn enough to support a family without the wife's income. Not so with blacks. Most black women have to work, and when they do, it is frequently as domestics and at other opportunities offering low pay. Also, their hours are long and inflexible, hardly allowing time-off for board meetings.

The white man who contributes his time to volunteer efforts has the resources of a secretarial staff and the certainty that his philanthropic forays in no way jeopardize his work with the firm, corporation, or profession. If anything, his volunteer activities enhance his business and social standing. The Board of Directors of the Legal Aid Society in New York City, for example, embraces that city's legal elite, who can attend the frequent meetings without worrying about "who's minding the store."

So what kinds of civic contacts are there between blacks and whites? Under pressure to look more representative, many formerly all-white philanthropies have "gone out and found one or two." The blacks they usually find are those employed in social-service-type work and whose jobs have required community contacts. Or if they are from the black "elite", they may be professionals with some flexibility in their schedules. But they usually lack the base of large back-up offices which have the resources and assured income to give them the luxury of giving unto others—without worry.

Black and White Together à la Poverty

That leaves us with poverty-type programs, governmentally or privately funded. Recall that the initiation of these programs followed a chain of ghetto riots. What happened was that the nation, not usually known for its future orientation, envisioned the rampaging black masses invading their streets. It was S.O.S. and S.O.P. (Save Our Skins and Save Our Property). Programs were born and with them, the white hopes for an end to long, hot summers.

Even in the days of "community control" and "maximum feasible participation", it was difficult for most whites to adjust to the notion of blacks being in charge of organizations that included whites. Perplexed, they would employ a number of devices to cope with this shift in the usual rules and would anxiously ask the black leaders-apparent about funding, boards of directors, investors, creditors, parent corporations—anything that might indicate that whites were in the background pulling the strings after all.

The white assumption that blacks could not exercise leadership in business, finance, government and international affairs bewilders most blacks, who for years have borne witness to government inefficiency, neglect, and inequity. Blacks simply feel it is impossible to do any worse than whites have done and that there is much to be said for a black Secretary of State who would be more understanding of the attitudes and feelings of the world's non-white majority and would invest foreign policy with a new humanism. What could be lost by trying?

GIVING UP THE GHOST

Some whites in the poverty scene have accepted the inevitability of relinquishing to blacks the control of those organizations advancing the interests of black people. Still, the transitional stages have posed difficulties, particularly for those slated to assume command. Even those whites with the best of conscious intentions have resisted the passing of the old order in countless subtle ways. Instructive is the transitional period of an anti-poverty organization which decided to have two directors, one black (incoming), the other white (outgoing) so that the transfer of power might be as smooth as possible. At meetings of the Board of Directors, each of the co-directors would report in turn on program developments and problems. When the white co-director spoke, comments and questions concerning what he had said were, appropriately, directed to him by name. When the black co-director reported, questions and comments on his report were *also* addressed to the white co-director, as though only he had the power of speech. Making matters worse, the white director, from time to time, would summarize the substance of the black director's statements, immediately after he had spoken, as if only he were believable to the largely white board. (See: "How to Avoid White Liberalism #2).

"BLACKER-THAN-THOU": THE WHITE BOUNTY

The reactions of a few "grassroots" blacks to the assumption of leadership by other blacks frequently reinforces the resistance of whites to the transfer of control. An old antipathy, originating in white created distinctions based upon color and education, still exists between the black educated and uneducated, despite the recent insistence that everything black is beautiful. Many lower-income blacks have experienced the double scorn of both whites and middle-income blacks and have been betrayed by both acting in their behalf. In some community-based organizations, the old antipathies have surfaced and aim at the black professional group—which, ironically, now that it has new options outside the black community, works in the ghetto primarily out of dedication. The blacker-than-thou-theme starts with him; he is accused of not being black enough. His manner of speaking, education, and professionalism type him as "white."

Whites who are privy to these internecine squabbles frequently assume that only grassroots persons are qualified to speak with authority on black problems and that *their* evaluations of black professionals are generally sound. If the black professional thus can't assume leadership in these organizations, then the obvious heirs are the grassrooters—and their white advisors. But even the most blacker-than-thou grassroots person will at *some* point acknowledge the need for technical assistance. With the black professionals ousted, he turns to the next obvious source of assistance. Thus white consulting firms wax profitably. Color them green.

In this kind of "collaboration", guess who's in control.

Schools: A Special Racial Case

Schools are a special racial case. Why?

They are *the* "social situation" promising the most contact between whites and blacks. Instead of brief and haphazard meetings, students see one another in classrooms, in laboratories, in gymnasiums, at club meetings after school, over lunch, and—under pressure.

Given the peculiar propensities of white American parents, any racial count-down on schools at the elementary or high school levels necessarily focuses on the *avoidance* of white-black contact rather than the contact.

Why talk about it then? Because *whites* need the contact. The current generation's fixation on and adoption of things black is striking evidence of the appeal and need.

In a time when America is lamenting "what's wrong", aware youngsters are turning to the closest source of inspiration: America's rich black culture, with its language, music, warmth, expansiveness, humor, and honesty.

Another reason to look at this "non-contact" is that it contains a quiet, hidden boomerang that is significant for white American family life. Read on.

America's pride in its free public education is legendary. It represents what Americans claim is indispensable to democracy. But as with too many American "traditions" like voting and the right to sit, stay, and live anywhere, blacks must prove and fight for their eligibility. Next to the threat which racial integration poses to this cherished tradition, the brief Sputnik furor pales. Race has become the 4th R.

Left to themselves, kids would naturally integrate. Racial distinctions are taught, along with good table manners, never talking to strangers, and making one's bed; for years, white parents have been running from blacks and barricading their precious ones against the carriers of darkness in segregated neighborhoods established and protected by federal mortgage guarantees and restrictive covenants.

An important Americanism has been the great distances children across the land have walked or ridden to school.

Now, of course, with talk of bussing to redress racial im-
balance, the little ones must be protected from such stren-
uous demands upon their energies. The sanctity of the
"neighborhood school" is the latest in the series of racial
dodges.

THE REASONS FOR "RUNNING"

Now why is the average white American parent willing to
fight to death to keep his little one from sitting next to a
darker little one in the classroom? Possibly because public
education is the foundation on which the American myth
that anybody can be everything is erected. Opportunity is
almost synonymous with education; it has been the key-
stone in the democratic bridge to wealth, power, or fame.
But despite reports on the number of new American mil-
lionaires, the fact is that there is little room at the American
top. Apart from a faint hope that a daughter or son at Yale
might marry money, somewhere the average white realizes
that academic achievement alone will not bring regular invitations to The Society Event of the Year. He scrambles
for whatever status is available and views little black children as a clear and present danger.

"JOHNNY WILL BE HELD BACK"

With those white parents who allowed the torment of
"integrated education" to reach any level of "rational"
verbalization there was a familiar litany against the idea.
They said first of all that they were concerned about standards, that Johnny would be held back by associating with
the "culturally deprived". Now what did these frantic parents mean by "held back?" Were they worried that with
the presence of allegedly mentally deficient blacks, their

children would never experience the joys of poetry, theo-
retical mathematics or philosophy? Were they concerned
that the classroom topics of debate would be limited? No.
Clearly, such parents were not especially concerned about
Johnny becoming an Einstein, an Oppenheimer, or a Paul-
ing. Most of these parents could not have cared less about
intellectual challenge, the development of the capacity to
think logically, debate intelligently, and to analyze cre-
atively with some modicum of objectivity. They anguished
over *their* white Johnny, in a classroom with blacks, falling
behind some other white Johnny who wasn't. In their
minds black kids meant the need for remedial attention
and less teacher time for their own little Johnny in his
competitive quest. These parents who mowed lawns, drank
beer and watched TV have wanted their children to get
degrees which could be marketed for dollars. Pure and simple, education meant cash, and blacks were a threat.

"They'll Teach Johnny Bad Things"
Then there was the "negative influence" argument. White
parents were worried that black-white exposure in schools
meant that white children would come under the corrupt-
ing influence of little black ones and learn about such
things as dirty words, sex, playing hooky, breaking rules,
stealing and fighting. Their objection, thus, was a moral
one. Black would infect white, and there would be
epidemics of juvenile delinquency.

The social objection against integrated schooling, rarely
phrased in a straight-forward way, was that these white parents might someday become not-so-adoring-grandparents of
not-so-white children. (See Interracial Dating and Marriage: "Getting Even").

THE RESULTS OF "RUNNING"

OK. So the parents fought, and in many instances "won." The children were quarantined against the black disease. Then what happened? These very same children emerged from their crystalline cocoons. Though the parents had staved off the blacks who would have held their youngsters back, white youngsters themselves started dropping out. Across the country they were leaving schools, colleges and universities without those much vaunted scrolls, and setting out towards the country's slums in search of relevance.

Curiously, despite their racial isolation, white youngsters developed their version of black language and started mumbling, talking hip and sounding inarticulate. Danny Thomas, that beloved father-comedian, hilariously lamented this development in a nationally televised spoof about him and his UCLA son trying to "communicate." The young Thomas, to his father's dismay, spoke in gestures and phrases: "yeah, man", "like you know", "like I gotta split", "like it's groovy man, let's make it." Billions of education dollars, including Danny Thomas', seemed to be drifting down the drain, if language was any sign at all. Suddenly Johnny couldn't talk!

In many instances (despite the absence of blacks as fellow students during their formative years), the protected white youth launched the country's first *violent* educational offensive. These students broke laws, imprisoned deans, destroyed property, and in more than a few instances were responsible for serious personal injuries. All without black instruction.

Oddly enough, without meeting "them" in gyms, lavatories, or at slumber parties, the little darlings somehow learned about "pot" "scag", and "speed." They were "turning on." What had been a black-only problem suddenly became a crisis in suburbia, with its neighborhood schools. Now that white kids were "shooting up" in Vietnam and at home, the President and others saw the problem as worthy of national attention. And after the sons of the late Robert F. Kennedy, New Jersey's Governor Cahill, and New York gubernatorial hopeful Howard Samuels— not to mention others—were arrested for violation of marijuana laws, it was time to lower the penalties.

In still more grievous ways, the parental prohibitions against contact with young Sambo boomeranged. Parents were at a loss about how their youngsters, reared on daily baths, washing behind the ears, shirts and shorts Tide-bright suddenly looked unkempt, and anything but the model of future General Motors executives. All this without contact with "those dirty, sloppy niggers"!!! White kids were also dressing "poor", declining the attire their parents connect with status.

Listening to Ray Charles, B. B. King, Bessie Smith, and James Brown, the kids got hooked on statement-suffering music, the soulful sound of blackness. Some of them even managed to sing and sound almost-black, which is the special appeal in the styles of Tom Jones, Janis Joplin, and Joe Cocker.

The white kids, without classroom contact with their black inferiors, then looked for alternatives to the asensual, sterile, hypocritical, wife-swapping morality of parental suburbia. They found them. Today, living together (for blacks, it was called "shacking up"), communal living (the equivalent to the black extended family?) and having children without benefit of marriage (called "illegitimacy" when blacks do it) seem to be those alternatives.

What brought all this on? The children were *protected* from the scourge of integration in the classroom. And blacks were not neighbors. Or fellow-worshippers. Or the sexy pin-ups or the gunslinging movie heroes.

But something clearly boomeranged. It would be too facile to say that the children came to yearn for the very things which had been so carefully prohibited. That may be a part of it—the "forbidden fruit" theme.

On a deeper level, the kids rejected the materialism, the "rat race," and the sterility of their parents' lives. They even rejected their parents.

In searching for alternatives, they looked at the blacks whom their parents rejected and who were testing the very ideals those parents had given only lip service to. The kids identified with the blacks, the underdogs, the outcasts. An idealism and a search for honest answers, which might otherwise have been starved in suburbia, found new sources of inspiration in the speeches of black leaders and in the black demonstrations against inequities. They compared the words of Martin Luther King Jr. with the "truths" in their own living rooms. They discovered that there were others who *felt* there was something askew in America. And they were black. Perhaps one didn't have to be white after all?

So you see, racial isolation in schools, neighborhoods, or elsewhere is no guarantee that such "protected" youngsters will emulate the middle American model uncritically.

Nothing has been gained by the massive resistance to racial integration in schools. In fact, America now has its first near-raceless generation. By not fighting the inevitable, white parents could gain the respect—perhaps more important than love—of their children. As their credibility gap closes, perhaps so will the generation gap.

Advice

All these social situations (the less personal ones) have a lot of themes in common. Blacks and whites find themselves meeting and brushing against one another impersonally. The exchanges are often brief, always in public settings, and frequently without the give-and-take that comes with people knowing one another. Without the expectation or hope of a black-white friendship, whites lapse into what might be called stock responses based on American folklore about blacks. Call them presumptions.

What's puzzling about all these presumptions is that they develop as full-blown and authoritative opinions despite the lack of black-white interaction and a good chance to test "theories."

How do whites know blacks? What are their contact points? Certainly not as neighbors on shady, tree-lined suburban lanes. Certainly not as classmates who stroll home from school together. Rarely as fraternity brothers planning the week-end panty raid (or sit-in?). Rarely as relatives. Sometimes as co-workers. Rarely as strategists in major political campaigns. Infrequently as bowling buddies. Seldom as pew-sharers. Only lately in adjacent tombs. Ever as box-owners at the Metropolitan? Never as spacemates en route to the moon. Uncommonly as business partners, Wall Street or Main Street. Never as media magnates.

So what's left? Those situations where there are the bosses and the bossed. And what can people know about each other in such roles? Very little.

Back to the themes. What are they? There is the "Poverty Presumption"; it surfaces in shopping. Then there is the "Enslavement Theme", applied to black domestics and diners. The "Rape and Robbery" presumption crops up when blacks shop, take taxis, or try to get an education. The "Stupidity-theme" rears its ugly little head around education and civic contacts. Finally, a trio of presumptions pervading almost all these less-personal black-white social situations: Uncouthness. Morality. Emotionalism, that volatile potential forever lurking just beneath the black surface. Or so it's feared.

These presumptions, admittedly numerous, are difficult to overcome. But consciousness can do it. To aid the highly motivated, this memory aid will keep the white alert to the white themes that offend blacks and make racial rapport impossible: Don't PRESUME. Remember, don't

P   OVERTY
R   "ROB 'N' RAPE"
E   NSLAVEMENT
S   TUPIDITY
U   NCOUTHNESS
M   ORALITY
E   MOTIONALISM

Get it?

These presumptions put blacks off.

As an aside, white preconceptions about black poverty, considering who hires and fires, are statistically likely. Nevertheless, it offends the individual black even if he is poor; the presumption tears to shreds his American dream.

4

Racial Refrains

The American song-and-dance routine called race has produced a host of white sayings. When blacks hear them their racial antennae go up. These stock phrases have a clear racial purpose in that they are rarely said by whites to whites. It is because they are reserved for blacks that they differ from "small talk" (see "Hob-nobbing") which covers those comments which *could* be neutral but become racially loaded in the black-white context.

The following refrains are anything but music to black ears. Because the well-meaning white would hardly figure out on his own why this is so, hopefully with these examples, he'll tune in.

"Some of my best friends are . . ."

"Negro" was the way it was put. (See Eeny-Meeny-Miny-Mo). Fortunately, one doesn't hear it much any more, but occasionally whites resort to it to reassure the black listener that they're really O.K. Racially, that is. The effect of such pronouncements is to stress that the contrary is more likely the case. Recall Shakespeare's truism: "Methinks the lady doth protest too much."

Blacks note that wealthy people are never heard to say that some of their best friends are poor. In the first place, no one need believe it, but if perchance someone did, they'd wonder what the point in mentioning it was. Brownie points? Sounds like it.

There is too much display in the claim. It runs counter to what friendship is all about, in the sense that the "friendships", if they exist at all, seem to be more for the public than for the people involved.

There are several limited contexts, however, where the "some of my best friends are black" sentiment is probably accurate. Whites seek out blacks, often their domestics, to air particularly intimate problems. This seems a part of what has been called the Mammy Syndrome. Since the black confidante does not share the total social life of these troubled whites, the blacks, by virtue of such social distance, are certain-to-be-silent sources of help.

There are, of course, further limits to the "best friends" phenomenon. First of all, as Dick Gregory said, "There simply ain't enough of us to go around" (being best friends with all those whites proclaiming it.)

Finally, it is significant that one would never hear a black say, "Some of my best friends are white." Wonder why?

"But the Irish (Jews, Italians, . . .) did it, why can't you?"

Whites are frequently given to drawing parallels between the American experiences of blacks and other immigrant groups. Black people are reminded that the Irish, Italians, and Poles came to these shores of opportunity and "made something of themselves" as a result of hard work and frugality. The implication, of course, is that if blacks had worked harder, their fate would have been different. One wonders, then, about the widespread use of the phrase, "worked like a nigger" to describe back-breaking effort.

Blacks resent such comparisons. No group ever worked harder in the service of building America. (Remember slavery?) So why are blacks still "last"? For all but the fairest blacks, the possibility of "melting" in the great American pot simply did not exist. Blacks could never get lost in the crowd, thus the slave stigma stuck. A Pole could change his name from Marciszewski to Muskie and become the father of a presidential hopeful. As yet, there are no bleaching agents strong enough to make a Jesse Jackson an Andrew Jackson.

Whites seem to think that blacks are recent arrivals. Several years ago at Brown University, this question was asked of the freshman class: "Which of you have both sets of grandparents born in the United States?" The lone black stood. What has happened is that in the fierce competition of the nineteenth and early twentieth centuries, blacks did not count. Laws and customs kept them out of the running. Only lately, as blacks have pressed their own claims for a piece of the action, have whites taken notice that they're even in the race.

Recent arrivals indeed!

"A credit to his race . . ."

Whites have had a way of choosing one Negro, liking him and holding him up as a model to all blacks. Joe Louis was one, Lionel Hampton another, and now Joe Frazier.

The phrase assumes that blacks need crediting or something to balance their dark doom. To become a "credit" one must be compliant, not challenge white judgment on anything at all, smile appropriately, and have some stardom in a limited area, usually sports or entertainment. Though the phrase is heard less often these days, the attitude remains.

Keeping in mind the notion of equality, whites should remember that blacks notice that there is no corresponding concept in whitedom. No one has ever called any white man a credit to his race. And blacks know that white baddies are not referred to as discredits or embarrassments to *their* race; *those* types are merely "bad men" or "bad people". As one black Virginia grandmother put it, "Nobody blamed Hitler on white folks."

Muhammad Ali's popularity in the black community is a part of all this. Smart, quick, witty and challenging, white people do not walk over him, though they tried more than once. They revoked his license to box, allegedly because his violation of the draft law made him a "bad example" for impressionable youth. It was conveniently overlooked, until Ali's lawyers pointed it out, that a substantial number of boxers had criminal records. O purest of sports!

Ali's defeat in March of 1971 was cheered by whites. In New York that night, a white truck driver for the New York *Daily News* was heard hollering to another, "Hey'd ya hear that nigger got beat?" In other words, there was only one of the two blacks fighting who deserved the pejorative term. The *other* represented docility and therefore reasonableness. To blacks, though, Joe Frazier was a throwback to the Joe Louis era when blacks "took it".

Having beat "an uppity nigger", Frazier was then qualified to speak before the august and racist body that is the South Carolina state legislature. He was the first black man to do so since Reconstruction. Noticed many boxers making legislative addresses lately? In white terms, Frazier is a credit to his race.

"What do you people want?"

Why does this one really get to blacks?

It assumes that it must be something different from what white people want. Assumption erroneous.

There's a haven't-you-got-enough premise underneath this question, and it suggests that blacks should be satisfied with less.

That's all.

"The first black to . . ."

Whites pat themselves on the back with this one. Letting-one-in is heralded as positive proof that there's a little bit of equality. Considering the praise and superlatives accompanying the Event, one wonders why the Perfect Man didn't achieve his reward much earlier.

In certain circumstances, this kind of fanfare would not be so bad; after all, important events merit trumpeting. But the hoopla here confirms the tokenism. It means that the event is indeed a special one and unlikely to happen as a regular matter.

Older blacks took great pride in the lone black stars who were in any way recognized or included in the white world. And those "stars" interpreted their singularity as a sign that they were inherently special and superior to other blacks. (See "Integration Index: Ready Richard.")

Younger blacks don't care about being the first or the only. They recognize that the only one of anything in any field is weak and vulnerable. They want company.

"How do you know . . . ? (Mr. or Mrs. White Person)"

The scene: white meets black with white friend of white. Or: white talks to black, discovers black knows white he knows. White soon asks black how he comes to know other white. Problem here: white knows whites usually know whites and blacks, blacks. How come cross-up?

The question is a recognition of usual racial lines and the inquiry seeks to pinpoint precisely how this black and that white managed to cross them.

It is noteworthy that whites ask, "How do you *know*

so-and-so?" rather than "How did you *meet* so-and-so?" "Meet" implies an ordinary, everyday happenstance. "Know", by contrast, suggests the momentous or the extraordinary. Perhaps it is for a black to know a white. Nevertheless, the question annoys blacks as still another reminder of racial lines.

"It's for your own good"

This refrain alerts blacks that whites are up to something. It says to the average black that the line or product or scheme the white is touting will benefit—guess who. It also implies that blacks don't know their own best interests—and that's insulting.

"Violence will get you nowhere"

Oh yeah? The greatest social strides for blacks recently have followed violent outbursts. Would that it were otherwise; how much more peaceful and pleasant it would be if the delegations, petitions, marches, prayers and vigils would bring dollars for darkies as quickly!

Black violence seems a special sort in the white mind. Although 94% of all white homicide victims are killed by other whites, it would be difficult to detect this fact from the way "crime in the streets" has been linked with blacks by the media.

It is not lost on blacks that when whites are serious about something they employ violence. The underworld and its protection rackets, labor conflicts and Vietnam all dispense with "discussion", "negotiations" and "peaceful protest".

Ye olde double standard!

"You're pushing too fast"

Black people aren't hearing this quite so much these days. Thank the Lord!

Where this refrain is still warbled, whites are asking blacks to time their quest for equality at a pace that is comfortable and convenient for whites.

Now rrrrreally! This is like Custer at Little Big Horn asking Sitting Bull to fight only at dawn and twilight so that the General could avoid sunburn. Would you?

"How come the others didn't make it?"

BLACK: Things are worse than they were ten years ago.

WHITE: How can you say that?

BLACK: Housing has deteriorated, unemployment has increased, there are more dropouts and drug addiction has gotten worse.

WHITE: (Pause) Really? (Thinking)

BLACK: Yeah.

WHITE: But look at you. You made it. Things can't be all that bad.

Typically, that's the way it goes.

Whites deny that things are as gloomy for black folks as they maintain. What whites seem to be saying is that if *anyone* can survive, things can't be all that bad for black people as a whole.

To the average black, such attitudes are akin to American soldiers arriving to liberate the survivors at a concentration camp and asking why the others died—since a few had obviously managed to survive.

Here again is the white view that blacks can endure more suffering and privation.

Because the white is talking to *this* black, something he may not have been doing a few years ago, he thinks there must be zillions more like him. And he's right in the sense that there are more who are making it. But the black birthrate being what it's been, there are also many more who are not.

Wrap-up

Whites do not consciously say these things to be mean, to hurt blacks, or to be racist. They say them mainly to encourage, reassure or to be what they consider helpful or friendly. Yet what comes through is their belief that, though blacks are no longer "three-fifths of a man", they aren't five-fifths either.

To call it naïveté is a bit generous. Rather, it seems that whites have an engrained need to turn away from the facts. A kind of self-protection operates here, for whites appear to believe that if they were truly to undo their black past, it might mean parting with too much.

How much is too much?

5

How to Avoid
White Liberalisms

This "white-liberal" business is a source of much confusion.
How can it be that the one white who sees himself as
meaning only the best towards blacks catches it? Basically,
the problem is what psychologists call "attitudinal." This
species, like most white Americans, draws limits for blacks
despite professing not to.

Liberals are those who most frequently talked about
"rights," "guarantees" and "the Constitution," but when
real tests arose were interested mainly in their painless im-
plementation. What hurt, it seems, was to have to go
beyond talk.

Appreciate the problems in these illustrations.

Liberalism #1: "It's not the same thing."

When blacks decided to go it alone in a number of private
or quasi-public organizations, whites promptly charged "re-

verse racism". Aware of their own racial sins, whites apparently assumed the worst when blacks gathered together. (It
was no accident that during slavery it was illegal for three
or more blacks to assemble.)

Whites overlook their own separatism in area after area
because when *they* do it, they consider it normal. When
blacks do it, pointing out that they are doing nothing that
whites don't do, whites nevertheless condemn it. Black
separatism is "different" somehow. "It's not the same
thing."

Few whites have protested that the casts of most Broadway plays are all-white; yet when the Negro Ensemble
Company was formed in 1965, Howard Taubman, a leading drama critic, felt compelled to criticize this
development as fostering racial separation in the arts. Few
whites have criticized Chambers of Commerce, Rotary
and Kiwanis Clubs and the Daughters (Sons) of the American Revolution for being all-white. The President of the
United States and other high government officials revel at
their all-white parties week after week, and no outcries are
heard about the separatist or anti-black flavor of such frol-
ics. Roger Wilkins, nephew of Roy Wilkins and former
Assistant Attorney General of the United States, finding
himself at one of these intrinsically all-white affairs, was a
solitary critic indeed:

> When it was all over, a number of men had tears in
> their eyes, even more had lifted hearts and spirits, but a
> few were so dispirited that they went upstairs to get
> drunk. We had just heard the President and Vice-Presi-
> dent of the United States in a unique piano duet—and
> to many Gridiron veterans, it was a moving show-stopper.
> To a few others, it was a depressing display of gross in-

sensitivity and both conscious and unconscious racism—
further proof that they and their hopes for their country
are becoming more and more isolated from those places
where America's heart and power seem to be moving.

The annual dinner of the Gridiron Club is the time
when men can put on white ties and tails and forget the
anxiety and loneliness that are central to the human con-
dition and look at other men in white ties and tails and
know that they have arrived or are still there.

The guests are generally grateful and gracious. But the
event's importance is beyond the structures of graciousness because it shows the most powerful elements of the
nation's daily press and all elements of the nation's government locked in a symbolic embrace. The rich and the
powerful in jest tell many truths about themselves and
about their country. I don't feel very gracious about what
they told me.

Some weeks ago, to my surprise and delight, a friend—
a sensitive man of honor—with a little half-apology, about
the required costume, invited me to attend the dinner.

The first impression was stunning: almost every passing
face was a familiar one. Some had names that were house-
hold words. Some merely made up a montage of the familiar faces and bearings of our times. There were Richard Helms and Walter Mondale and Henry Kissinger and
George McGovern and Joel Broyhill and Tom Wicker
and William Westmoreland and John Mitchell and Tom
Clark (ironically placed, by some pixie no doubt, next to
each other on the dais) and Robert Finch and Ralph
Nader, and of course, the President of the United States.

One thing quickly became clear about those faces.
Apart from Walter Washington—who, I suppose, as
Mayor had to be invited—mine was the only face in a
crowd of some 500 that was not white. There were no
Indians, there were no Asians, there were no Puerto Ri-

cans, there were no Mexican-Americans. There were just the Mayor and me. Incredibly, I sensed that there were few in the room who thought that anything was missing.

There is something about an atmosphere like that that is hard to define, but excruciatingly easy for a black man to feel. It is the heavy, almost tangible, clearly visible, broad assumption that in places where it counts, America is a white country. I was an American citizen sitting in a banquet room in a hotel which I had visited many times. (My last occasion for a visit to that hotel was the farewell party for the white staff director and the black deputy staff director of the United States Commission on Civil Rights.) This night in that room, less than three miles from my home in the nation's capital, a sixty-per-cent black city, I felt out of place in America.

This is not to say that there were not kind men, good men, warm men in and around and about the party, nor is it to say that anyone was personally rude to me. There were some old friends and some new acquaintances whom I was genuinely glad to see. Ed Muskie, who had given a very funny and exquisitely partisan speech (the Republicans have three problems: the war, inflation, and what to say on Lincoln's Birthday), was one of those. I was even warmly embraced by the Deputy Attorney General, Mr. Kleindienst, and had a long conversation with the associate director of the FBI, Mr. DeLoach.

But it was not the people who so much shaped the evening. It was the humor amidst that pervasive whiteness about what was going on in the country these days that gave the evening its form and substance. There were many jokes about the "Southern strategy." White people have funny senses of humor. Some of them found something to laugh about in the Southern strategy. Black people don't think it's funny at all. That strategy hits men where they live—in their hopes for themselves and their dreams for their children. We find it sinister and frightening. And let it not be said that the Gridiron Club and its guests are not discriminating about their humor. There was a real sensitivity about the inappropriateness of poking fun that night at an ailing former President, but none about laughing about policies which crush aspirations of millions of citizens of this nation. An instructive distinction, I thought.

There was a joke about the amendments to the Constitution (so what if we rescind the First Amendment, there'll still be twenty-five left), and about repression (you stop bugging me, I'll stop bugging you), and there were warm, almost admiring jokes about the lady who despises "liberal Communists" and thinks something like the Russian Revolution occurred in Washington on November 15th.* There was applause—explosive and prolonged—for Judges Clement Haynsworth and Julius Hoffman (the largest hands of the evening by my reckoning).

As I looked, listened, and saw the faces of those judges and of the generals and of the admirals and of the old members of the oligarchies of the House and Senate, I thought of the soft, almost beatific smile of Cesar Chavez, the serious troubled face of Vine Deloria, Jr., and the handsome, sensitive faces of Andy Young and Julian Bond of Georgia. All those men and more have fought with surely as much idealism as any general ever carried with him to Saigon, with as much courage as any senator ever took with him on a fact-finding trip to a Vietnam battlefield, or even as much hope, spirit, and belief in the American dream as any Peace Corps kid ever took to the Andes in Peru. But the men I have named fought for American freedom on American soil. And they were not there. But Julius Hoffman was.

* Moratorium Day, protesting the Vietnam War.

As the jokes about the "Southern strategy" continued, I thought about the one-room segregated schoolhouse where I began my education in Kansas City. That was my neighborhood school. When they closed it, I was bused— without an apparent second thought—as a five-year-old kindergartener, across town to the black elementary school. It was called Crispus Attucks.

And I thought of the day I took my daughter when she was seven along the Freedom Trail in Boston, and of telling her about the black man named Crispus Attucks who was the first American to die in our revolution. And I remember telling her that white America would try very hard in thousands of conscious and unconscious ways both to make her feel that her people had no part in building America's greatness and to make her feel inferior. And I remember the profoundly moving and grateful look in her eyes and the wordless hug she gave me when I told her, "Don't you believe them, because they are lies." And I felt white America in that room in the Statler-Hilton telling me all those things that night, and I told myself, "Don't you believe them, because they are lies."

And when it came to the end, the President and the Vice-President of the United States, in an act which they had consciously worked up, put on a Mister Bones routine about the Southern strategy with the biggest boffs coming as the Vice-President affected a deep Southern accent. And then they played their duets—the President playing his songs, the Vice-President playing "Dixie," the whole thing climaxed by "God Bless America" and "Auld Lang Syne." The crowd ate it up. They roared. As they roared I thought that after our black decade of imploring, suing, marching, lobbying, singing, rebelling, praying, and dying we had come to this: a Vice-Presidential Dixie with the President as his straight man. In the serious and frivolous places of power—at the end of that decade—America was still virtually lily white. And most of the people in that room were reveling in it. What, I wondered, would it take for them to understand that men also come in colors other than white? Seeing and feeling their blindness, I shuddered at the answers that came readily to mind.

As we stood voluntarily, some more slowly than others, when the two men began to play "God Bless America," I couldn't help remembering Judy Collins (who could not sing in Chicago*) singing "Where Have All the Flowers Gone?"

So later I joined Nick Kotz, author of *Let Them Eat Promises*, and we drank down our dreams.

I don't believe that I have ever been blanketed in and suffocated by such racism and insensitivity since I was a sophomore in college and was the only black invited to a minstrel spoof put on at a white fraternity house.

But then, they were only fraternity brothers, weren't they?

Most whites nevertheless persist and argue that their form of separatism is different from the black one. For whites, the "difference," if any, seems to lie only in the fact that blacks are doing it.

In late 1966, the American Jewish Committee, disturbed by the decisions of CORE and SNCC to become all black, convened a meeting of young black and Jewish professionals to see whether a "dialogue" was still possible between those of similar achievements. When the whites condemned the new direction of SNCC and CORE, the blacks quietly asked how the policies of these newly all black organizations differed from those of the American Jewish Committee itself. The blacks pointed out that

* At the 1968 Democratic National Convention.

the American Jewish Committee restricted membership to "Jews, their spouses and children who are citizens of the United States." The young Jewish professionals argued that AJC was "different" because Judaism was a religion and that just as Catholics and Baptists and others organized, so did Jews.

The blacks pointed out that in the AJC, people had not come together primarily for purposes of worship; that it was not a religious corporation, but, rather, organized to advance the human, social and civic interests of a people with a common culture and heritage. By that measure, SNCC and CORE did not differ.

When the dialogue reached the "what can we do" stage, the blacks proposed that maids be paid the minimum wage and that rent-controlled apartments (gems in New York City) vacated by whites be referred to blacks. The whites resisted each, and the AJC staff member, realizing that the situation was beyond their control, closed this series of "dialogues" by noting that perhaps AJC would meet with other (more cooperative?) blacks in the future.

On another level, however, there is a real difference in the two colors of separatism. They spring from different sources. The black version is a *response* to the white one, not an equivalent. After years of taking it, blacks reached a point and said, "Enough!" No longer willing to accept the daily assaults on their dignity which whites imposed under their version of separatism, blacks opted for psychological distance.

How do whites avoid this "it's not the same thing" liberalism? They must no longer "require" of blacks what they don't require of themselves. Consistency is the watchword here. When the private and quasi-public organizations of

whites are fully open, there will be less need for black counterparts.

Liberalism #2: "We only want to help."

Liberals have been called "bleeding hearts"; they seek to
help the down-trodden, underprivileged, and oppressed. In
America, guess who that's meant.

In all too many instances, through a strange transformation, the "help" has turned into domination. Particularly
when blacks show signs of wanting to be their own masters,
the liberal desire to control surfaces. It is as though the
"help" never contemplated the full independence and self-
reliance of blacks.

In 1967, a white architectural and urban planning organization in Harlem saw the necessity of adding blacks to
the staff. In existence for approximately two years, it had
been staffed by five white architects and one black, a secretary. In response to pressure from community and funding
sources, the white director decided to handpick two blacks,
a lawyer and an architect who was named co-director. Several months of eventless integration passed before black
staff members, used extensively for those assignments in-
volving community contact, discovered that their organization lacked credibility in Harlem because of its white
image. They thus proposed that the Harlem office
eventually become all black and that the white director re-
locate himself outside the community and devote his time
to fund-raising and informing whites of conditions in Harlem. His salary would continue to be paid by the organiza-

tion, while his rent would come from one of several consultantships he had wangled while heading the Harlem office. The all-white board of directors was enlarged to include a majority of Harlem residents; also, several white staff positions were to be phased out over a six-month period of time.

The transformation appeared to have been accomplished neatly, without acrimony or resentment.

The board members gathered for their first meeting. They were now an expanded and predominantly black board. Prior to the meeting, a number of the blacks gathered around the director's desk, now occupied by the black co-director, to discuss the feasibility of community sponsored low-income housing projects for Harlem, a major focus of the organization since its inception. The white director-emeritus arrived. During his tenure he had spent a great deal of time analyzing the difficulties of such a program but had nevertheless become a strong advocate of such projects, with the organization shepherding proposals through the multiple levels of administrative approval.

The scene as he entered the office: the new black director comfortably discussing the diverse technical aspects of low-income housing sponsorship, the black staff members and new board members commenting. 'Twas a traumatic scene indeed!

For several moments, white-emeritus seemed hypnotized. When he spoke, his tone of voice suggested anything but good will. Curiously, he now enumerated *all* the possible obstacles to the success of such projects, including those difficulties which he had, in the past, minimized. When the blacks informed him that they had already considered those very obstacles, he adamantly insisted that what they were proposing was extremely difficult and required more expertise than any of them as yet possessed.

The liberal, like white-emeritus, thinks he can do it better. In one sense he is right, because many of the whites with whom blacks ultimately have to deal are quicker to respond to another white. At the Harlem organization, both directors were Harvard graduates, but the white one, though with lesser credentials, probably would have had an easier time with the various FHA officials involved in getting approval for a housing project.

The liberal acting on behalf of the black is frequently aware of such distinctions and uses them to justify his taking charge of just about everything; he uses racism to consolidate his position of control.

More subtly, what the liberal hates most is being irrelevant to blacks, for over the years he had made them the tip of his liberal bayonet. Before consumerism and ecology emerged to fill the void, he realized that without the black thrust his liberal joustings seemed blunted.

Blacks don't need such "assistance." They find that an FHA-type white functionary, once he recovers from the shock of black literacy, assumes black articulateness to mean a full knowledge and willingness to pursue the enforcement of anti-discrimination remedies. The result? He does his job and the black accomplishes his purpose.

Blacks, like anyone, however, welcome help. What is resented are white attempts to direct and dominate. Blacks are establishing their own goals and objectives, and any help from whites must be in those terms.

Liberalism #3: ". . . if he's qualified."

The words "qualifications" and "qualified" suddenly crop up when the advent of blacks is a possibility. It re-sembles a reflex reaction: in universities, on Wall Street, in industry, in the media, the inevitable response is, "Yes, of course, if he is qualified."

The deliberate denial of opportunities to blacks is a matter of history. Even so, a crazy faith prevailed among blacks leading them to assume that if they in fact became qualified, opportunities would appear. For years it has been a bitter joke that the United States Post Office has been a graveyard for black Ph.D's. It was one of the few places in the country where merit alone was a basis for employment —if a person passed a civil service test, he was assured a position sorting letters and carrying mail the rest of his life. Washington is a predominantly black city today for the same reasons: blacks were able to obtain reasonably well-paying jobs through competitive examinations in the civil service system. Wherever merit was the sole determinant of being hired, blacks have abounded.

The exclusion of blacks by American business and industry has been the starkest; for years, the corporation was a closed club. Whites made the trip from office boys to board chairmen frequently; no special skills were needed. Getting in was the key. After that, a shrewd blend of intelligence, hard work and apple-polishing took one into those plush executives suites. (Even today a range of interesting and high-paying job possibilities are available to whites without college degrees; yet the only route touted for blacks is to "get a degree".)

Those blacks who thought of trying to "qualify" met roadblocks in unlikely places, like school counselling offices. The "guidance" steered able blacks towards pursuits primarily menial and manual. Most blacks have a friend or two who managed to apply to, get admitted or finish college despite the urgent advice of white advisors. Ronald Davenport, the very black dean of the predominantly white Duquesne Law School, was advised in eighth grade by his white counselor that truck-driving should be his highest aspiration.

The same "counselors" obviously gave different advice to white students, justifying the advice to blacks out of an avowed concern for their ability to perform or "practicality." It was as though only whites were entitled to be ordinary. The middles and bottoms of classes in major universities, the middle and bottom standings of athletic teams for years were occupied by whites only. Businesses hired and fired *average* whites and rarely discussed "standards" and "qualifications" in so doing. The only test was whether they could do the job, and that could be known, oddly enough, only *after* hiring. It is curious to note how many of the old athletes honored today are white in sports which now include many black players. Could it be that blacks have developed athletic proficiency only since Jackie Robinson?

Nowadays, as more than a token number of blacks are entering this and that, whites react as though the floodgates have opened and the hue and cry about "qualifications" has reached a new high in decibels.

A major New York law firm, when questioned about its failure to hire more black attorneys, replied that it had hired two (the firm numbered well over one hundred attorneys) who "had not worked out too well." In other words, all black attorneys presumably would be like the two who had not worked out. Clearly, the firm would never have reached the same conclusion about white lawyers on the basis of its experience with two, or even ten, or fifty of them for that matter. If such were the case, there would be no white law firms at all.

Even on a public level the relevancy of qualifications differs for blacks and whites. No one thought Bobby Kennedy had been the nation's best lawyer and for that reason appointed Attorney General. Consider the reaction if Julian Bond, as President of the United States, appointed his brother James to the same spot. And large majorities of white voters, the same people otherwise obsessed with "qualifications", elected Ronald Reagan, the cowboy, George Murphy, the movie hoofer, and Lester Maddox, the axe-wielder, to high public office. Imagine the stir over "qualifications" and "experience" if Sidney Poitier or Sammy Davis, Jr. ran for the California governorship or the United States Senate seat.

With all the agonizing, the trickle of blacks into previously all-white or predominantly white domains has not been accompanied by the collapse of those institutions. While it is true that American business has been in the throes of an especially persistent recession, it is doubtful that anyone, not even the most "qualified" white, would blame it on the newly hired black executives.

Why is this a liberal problem? Because he at least takes the first step and says, "Yes, of course" that blacks (or more accurately, a black) should be included; yet his speedy emphasis on the need to maintain standards exposes his abiding ambivalence about blacks invading his long exclusive domains. The liberal differs here from the more frankly anti-black run-of-the-mill American in that he is embarrassed about wanting to preserve his privileges and hides behind a concern for quality.

Solution: the liberal must watch for these themes and take note whenever words like "standards" or "qualified" roll off his lips in reference to blacks. Difficult though it may be, he must try to substitute "white" for "black" in all these instances and see how he would come out. The liberalism we are concerned about here would disappear with just this consciousness.

Liberalism #4: "Try to be objective."

Liberals assume that because they are white they are more objective about race than blacks. They think that all but the most white-oriented Negro spokesmen have an axe to grind, that blacks have a stake in exaggerating things, and that race paranoia is rampant among blacks. They feel that the black cannot fully appreciate his situation, that he is "too sensitive", "'too ideological", "polemical" or "doesn't take all the factors into consideration". In short, "non-objective."

Liberals are most sympathetic about this problem that they see in blacks. So they consolingly urge their darker brethren: "Try to be objective."

Now really! What liberals seem to forget is that blacks did not create the race problem. Not one anti-miscegenation law, grandfather clause restricting who could vote, anti-bussing decision, zoning ordinance, preventive detention proposal, racially restrictive covenant or union membership limitation, was dreamed up by blacks. Can it be that those who created the problem are more objective than blacks, who've borne the brunt?

Why do whites insist that blacks are not objective? Seems a case of seeing in others that which dwells within oneself. Projection? Alas!

ALL THE NEWS THAT FITS

The news does not report itself. Events do not come forth and speak. Mostly, white journalists do. How objective have they been? Not very, particularly when reporting controversial racial events. A Columbia University study on minority news coverage bared some well-kept secrets about "objectivity". The New York liberal press' reactions to the demonstrations undertaken and planned by the late Dr. Martin Luther King, Jr., shows objectivity depended upon how far away the demonstrations were. The editorial stand *against* King's northern civil rights demonstrations was as strong as the support of southern ones. Perhaps distance made for objectivity.

The same study pointed out that *The New York Times* quoted Roy Wilkins' denunciations of black racism *twice* as frequently as his condemnations of white racism. Now which is the greater problem? In the same paper, so the study said, on controversial racial issues whites involved usually get quoted, while the blacks normally get summarized or paraphrased. And there is plenty of coverage of white backlash as a reaction to black pressure. But riots, which are really black backlashes, are rarely discussed as *reactions* to white oppression. The Columbia study also exposed how the New York media identified black organizations or people alleged to be bigoted while leaving bigoted whites anonymous. For example, a white science teacher at a New York high school was quoted as saying, "I think if the black people don't get into line, then we'll either have to annihilate or neutralize them." No name, no address, no shoe size here. After all, he was white. Would that Huey Newton, Angela Davis and Eldridge Cleaver were so protected—in the name of objectivity!

Look at who gets assigned to write what. One would think that because black reporters are "non-objective" about race, they would be deployed to report and analyze national and international events which were non-racial: the war crimes of Lieutenant Calley, the Army scandal of generals pilfering from PX's around the world, Patricia Nixon's wedding, or the lecture tours of Spiro Agnew. But they're not. Black reporters write mainly about race; but even then, if the racial event is controversial enough, by-lines are usually white.

The Ocean Hill-Brownsville School decentralization controversy in Brooklyn, New York, is a prime example of how black reporters, though usually hired for racial reasons, are seldom allowed to fully present the black point of view in white-black conflicts. The predominantly white, heavily Jewish United Federation of Teachers was pitted against a black and Puerto Rican community; there were charges of white racism and counter-charges of black anti-semitism. The *New York Times* dispatched a team of black reporters ostensibly to get the black side of the story, but no articles by them appeared. Instead, day after day, as the struggle lengthened into weeks, news of the battle and UFT teachers' strike was reported and analyzed by two Jewish reporters, Leonard Buder and Fred Hechinger. Now how "objective" could they have been? In the process, the black reporters suffered a serious loss of credibility with blacks in Ocean Hill-Brownsville who had divulged important information in the expectation that their side of the story would also be presented. Since the issues revolved around whether blacks had been fair to whites and whether whites were responding non-racially to blacks, the blacks were outraged when their position was ignored or relegated to some obscure corner of the newspaper or a however-paragraph at the end of an article.

The white faith in their unfailing ability to be objective about race results in their automatically assuming a white civil rights spokesman to be more credible. What looks like objectivity is an unspoken understanding that another white will rarely go beyond tokenisms in aiding blacks. Any white who tramples cherished premises while advancing black rights meets abuse and scorn. Recall Father Groppi, who was really serious about Milwaukee open housing. Another near-traitor would be Jane Fonda if she were to focus all her lovely protest energies on a single black issue.

It's funny. Even when the liberal press intends to be genuinely complimentary, certain predispositions are revealed in what they choose to focus on. When blacks are profiled, along with an account of family, animals and hobbies, will be some mention of style of dress wherein the adjectives "neat", "fashionable", "dapper", "mod", "conservative", or the like appear. One also sees "mild-mannered" and "soft-spoken." Such descriptions, usually omitted in describing whites, reveal the prevailing impression that the average black is anything but.

With more serious issues, the lack of objectivity is also glaring. The media have picked up on "the stupidity theme." The choice of terms to describe the anti-establishment leaders of both races is instructive. Newspapers consistently describe whites as "radical" and blacks as "militant"; rarely is it the other way round. The term "radical" presupposes an informed political framework within which an extreme position is maintained. "Militancy", on the other hand, implies the use of pressure, force, violence; it denotes nothing with respect to a political philosophy. Here again, we have "brains" (white) versus "brawn" (black).

ARTISTIC REVIEWS; JUDGMENTS

There are few exempt areas. Even art criticism reflects the white difficulty with being objective. Black painter, Romare Bearden, might be cubistic or a black dramatist like Douglas Turner Ward in the tradition of the theatre of the absurd; yet, only a few white reviews discuss their efforts in the context of the larger genre. It is as though the color of the artist or of his subjects automatically places the work outside established genres—abstract expressionism, socialist realism, surrealism, whatever. The refusal to accord any universality to a black artistic statement results in many critics comparing blacks only to other blacks; they are unable to see the black experience as a human experience. (But there are some black artists who, for a variety of reasons— mainly ideological—like the company the critics would have them keep and enjoy being compared to their friends.)

Many black artists take their material—dialogue, subjects, characters—from the familiar lower stratum of black life where the tone and texture are earthy and turbulent. However, even though the few celebrated white American playwrights—O'Neill, Miller and Albee—write in this style, the types of black efforts that critics seemingly have special difficulty with are these gutsy, no-holds-barred works in the realistic vein. It is instructive that the highly allegorical *Invisible Man* by Ralph Ellison, with its classical restraint and cool rendering of a black man's search for justice in America, is one of the few works which some white critics will concede has universal significance.

With the likes of Ellison, whenever credit is given to black talent, it is inevitably described as non-black. When discussing Ellison, whites often say that he should not be regarded as a "black writer", as though by writing something they liked or understood, he had transcended the state of being black. In America, where all writers are simply called "writers", not to be known as a black writer can only mean a transformation into a white one. This metamorphosis is quite similar to the old white Southern practice of eulogizing a faithful black servant at graveside. They would bestow upon him what they considered to be the highest form of praise: "Ol' Jeb was a *white* man. May God rest his soul."

Several themes emerge when whites review black works. If the particular creation shows blacks suffering, wallowing, wailing, or mad, white reviewers seem comfortable and more prepared to accept the movie or play as legitimately black, whatever that is. (With black painting, however, similar depictions are cited as evidence of the limited vision of the artist.) A white *New York Times'* reviewer of "For the Love of Ivy" lamented the movie's failure to explicitly render the "seething anger" of blacks. Another review criticized "Cotton Comes to Harlem", a movie many blacks found hilariously familiar, on the ground that the movie said "little about the Black Experience."

Such responses may be understandable, given the media's recent emphasis on black deprivation, anger, and open confrontation with whites. On another level, whites appear strangely reassured—in art as in life—when blacks spout hostility, rage, hopelessness, frustration, or bitterness. Blacks blandly or mirthfully going about their daily affairs seems to cause white distress. Perhaps what whites prefer, even "objective" white reviewers, is the angry black gesture confirming that they—whites—are still central to the black psyche and consciousness.

There is another curiosity of color here. One finds blacks reviewing black works, whites reviewing white works, whites reviewing black works, but hardly ever blacks reviewing white works in the newspapers and periodicals of general circulation. Such was the case with William Styron's book. Out of the approximately 55 reviews of his *Confessions of Nat Turner,* not a single black reviewed that white-heralded work of musings about *the* most significant American *slave* leader.

Interestingly, white books—even on black subjects—are reviewed in far more papers and journals than best-sellers written by blacks. Eldridge Cleaver's *Soul on Ice* merited fewer than half the number of reviews received by Styron's "Confessions." Pourquois???

CRITICISM—WITH AND WITHOUT RHETORIC

Some white critics and editors *claim* to want enlightened and objective black analysis without rhetoric. As Anatole Broyard put it in a *New York Times* review:

The black man's rhetoric is one of the things that make it difficult for well-meaning whites to talk to him today. It

goes without saying that he has earned the right to rhetoric: like jazz, it is a natural expression of his feelings
. . . whites and blacks will never be able to act together—
to really integrate the two races—*until we stop segregating
black writing and black rhetoric from analysis and criticism.* While the black experience belongs only to blacks,
the truth belongs to everybody. (emphasis added)

By Broyard's standards, what of the following exchanges?
In June, 1970, an article by Martin Gottfried entitled "Is
All Black Theatre Beautiful? No." in the *New York Times*
provoked a number of strong reactions from black writers
and critics. Perhaps in anticipation of the storm, the editor
at the end of the article promised a reply the next week by
black playwright and critic, Clayton Riley. What was
shocking to black readers was that the liberal *New York
Times* would print Gottfried's irrational outpourings.

During the following weeks, a number of letters commenting on both the Gottfried and the Riley articles were
published in the "Drama Mailbag", a section reserved for
letters to the editor. The published letters by blacks were almost uniformly emotional or inarticulate reactions. The
Times, despite its advance approval of the idea, later refused to publish a well-reasoned critique by a black critic
which took both the Gottfried article and the Riley response to task. Instead, the editor of the Arts and Leisure
Section took the time to *personally* reply to that letter,
suggesting that its references to the Jewish influence in the
New York theater were anti-semitic. Why was the detached
and lucid analysis by a black, cutting through the rhetoric
of Gottfried and Riley, rejected? Could it be that white
editors are comfortable mainly with black writing (or behavior) which is raging and rhetorical?

The three articles follow without comment. Together they raise important issues on race and criticism.

Is All Black Theater Beautiful? No

BY MARTIN GOTTFRIED

In trying to be racially relevant, the theater is tearing at its own guts. It is caught in a bind, pulled one way by a sense of racial crisis, the other way by objective standards of quality. Overcome by black urgency, eager for black approval, impelled by a desire to be involved in contemporary problems—and to do something about them—intimidated by the idea that only blacks can write about blacks (in fact, intimidated by black militancy in general), the theater has given in to artistic racism.

Professional and artistic standards are being compromised for the sake of black plays, playwrights and actors; standards of writing, production, performance and judgment are being lowered for blacks and it is prejudice all over again, inverse this time. If this can be defended as a sort of Head Start project, (a) does a Head Start project belong in a form of art, (b) isn't it condescending, (c) do lowered standards encourage or restrict artistic development and (d) if they are incubative, why is the Negro Ensemble Company (a beneficiary of relaxed standards), for example, still operating at a subprofessional level?

*

The Negro Ensemble Company is a phenomenon. If it weren't for the American racial mess, it wouldn't even exist. Its justification is its blackness, not its theater. If it weren't for the headlong rationalizations of the white liberal community, the company would be considered worthwhile at best. Because of the racist traditions of our theater, the company is serving a brutal need in giving black playwrights, directors and actors a place to work—encouragement to work—that they could never get elsewhere. It gives black audiences a theater that isn't white-downtown (though it is black-downtown). These things, fortunate and unfortunate, are true. Yet, to judge by its reception, the Negro Ensemble Company has presumably been presenting well-written, well-produced, well-acted plays, getting better all the time (the company's current financial crisis is irrelevant—it is common to all non-profit theaters).

With only some exceptions ("Song of the Lusitanian Bogey" by Peter Weiss, for one), that reception was unearned. Most of the plays have been amateurishly written and produced. Though the company has found three extraordinary men (in director Michael A. Schultz, designer Edward Burbridge and composer Coleridge-Taylor Perkinson), it has been able to gather and train only a few satisfactory actors despite years of ensemble experience. The NEC has suffered from overpraise and from the assumption that its blackness gives it a special reason to exist, whether or not the work is good. The company is admirably earnest in its purpose but its qualities are social rather than artistic, and it rattles between a fear of being too militant for the moderates and too moderate for the militants. The white public condescends to it and the black public is lured on by its primitively parochial level, not very different from that of old Yiddish theater.

One might assume that the Negro Ensemble Company, being the most famous of the country's black theaters, would get the best of the black scripts. That's just not the way things have worked out. LeRoi Jones, the most experienced, most poetic, most imaginative black playwright in the country, has never had a play produced there. Ed Bullins, perhaps our most promising black playwright, hasn't worked at the NEC either, but at the American Place Theater.

*

The American Place Theater is a *white* theater whose director, Wynn Handman, has been presenting at least one black play a season. Ironically, it is just such a sense of responsibility that is causing the problem.

Ordinarily, and certainly at the American Place—one of the most admirable theaters in the country—the only basis for play selection is artistic quality. When a director like Handman implicitly uses blackness as a criterion for even one play a season, he subverts his artistic standards to social ones. Handman is perfectly aware of a possible conflict between social and artistic values. He has simply decided that there are times when social needs come first; that a theater, to be vital, must respond to the world in which it exists; that the energy of black playwrights' commitment and the relevance of their plays make them, as he says, "voices worth hearing."

Some of his choices (Bullins's "The Electronic Nigger") have been consistent with the American Place Theater's artistic standards. Others (Charlie Russell's "Five on the Black Hand Side") have been embarrassingly naïve, inviting benign and almost colonial approval from Handman's overwhelmingly white subscription audiences.

Here, then, is the dilemma: how to do the best plays one can find (an artistic obligation) while doing black plays (a social obligation). But what if the best plays one finds do not include a black play? Should one sacrifice a superior "white" play for the sake of a "black" one because it is important to produce one black play a season or because *dues are owed?* I think the answer is clear—the only measure of a play's value is its quality.

The limitation to a black play mirrors the limitations black playwrights have placed upon themselves. Because of the way things are, they feel compelled to write about black people and the racial situation. On one hand, this compulsion—and the intensity of black anger—gives their plays a special drive. On the other hand, it is a restriction on content that deprives these writers of an independent existence as artists. It encourages propaganda and inevitably leads to agit-prop plays. Moreover, whether the style is naturalistic or cartoon, the plays invariably work out of ethnic mannerisms—the jargon, the gestures, the music of the ghetto. The black public is lured to this as a sophisticated theater experience when it is actually black mass-appeal entertainment, reinforcing ghetto values, written down to them by playwrights who have escaped that ghetto. Most of the plays are situation melodramas, redefined as reflecting *the contemporary black experience*. In fact, the only new black play I've seen that is involved with young, modern, intelligent black men—the only one that grapples maturely with the militant movement—is Bullins's "The Pig Pen" currently at the American Place Theater.

Ironically, Bullins—like so many black militants—is convinced that intellectual and cultural refinement (which it took to write "The Pig Pen") is white and that a black man who sounds educated is trying to be white. Through such thinking, black playwrights write purposely coarse dramas, stereotyped in a way not very different from television's "Amos 'n' Andy" (a victim of rote liberalism that would surely be produced by the Negro Ensemble Company and acclaimed as beautifully black were it written today by a black playwright).

There are also new versions of the *coon show*—black folks singin' and dancin'. Not since "Carmen Jones," that bitter reminder of 1940's liberalism, had anyone dared proɪuce an all-black show for Broadway consumption. The all-black "Hello, Dolly!" was appalling, all the more so for its success. What does "Dolly" have to do with black people? Nothing, of course. Why were the characters—*all* of them—black? It was a "Dolly" in blackface with no concern for the style or sense of the show. It was also hypocritical, cast exclusively with black actors when only token blacks had shown up in any of the white versions. The first qualification wasn't ability but race—and that, if nothing else, was a violation of the Fair Employment Practices Act. Would Jewish actors and audiences appreciate an *all-Jewish* "Dolly"?

*

"Dolly" wasn't the only recent coon show. There have been more each season ("Purlie" and "Billy Noname" most recently), flecked here and there with reference to black beauty, sit-ins and militancy, but existing essentially to merchanise black bodies—have them on stage as a color motif, a racial motif.

Yet we are pretending to be color blind, denying the effect that an all-black cast has on a white audience. This is no different from insisting that stage nudity has no emotional effect. The white reaction to black people is so fraught with emotional and environmental conditioning that the very presence of a black man, on or off stage, sets off a series of reactions we haven't even begun to understand. It is the awareness of these reactions that makes black people distrust all white men, and it is stupid for theater people to shut their eyes to this when the reaction of spectator to performance is at the very heart of theater.

The plain fact is that the New York stage—its producers, its creators, its audiences, its whole point of view —is white. Its color hang-ups, racism and efforts at self-reform could not be more typical of the well-meaning (but conservative and suppressive) liberal community. Our theater is as white as our country, and the black man feels like and is treated like an alien there, just as he is in America. This whiteness of our theater turns *any* black production into a coon show because it puts black culture into a case in a white exhibition hall. The confrontation of a white theatergoer with a stageful of black actors may at last put him in *some* vaguely personal situation with a black man, but no matter how angry a black play may be, the white environment turns it sour—makes it into a display of black wares in the white marketplace and invites a kind of visiting benevolence.

These complex relationships—the racial gap—prevent white audiences from being natural toward black plays. The fear of misunderstanding makes misunderstanding only more likely. The result has been jittery white reactions to even the best of recent black plays, like "No Place to Be Somebody."

*

Charles Gordone's play was a disorganized mixture of gangster movie melodrama, poetry, set pieces and surrealism. Parts of it were very impressive and Gordone is an extremely talented playwright, but his play is also long, clumsy and confused. Yet, it was so extravagantly praised that it was moved out of the laboratory at Joseph Papp's Public Theater and into a large off-Broadway house, ultimately winning the Pulitzer Prize—that dependable barometer of middle-class ideas. What Papp had correctly analyzed as a fascinating play that needed a protected environment for additional work was overpraised into a major production. The play simply wasn't that good. If it hadn't been black, this situation would never have occurred. Gordone deserved better.

Such overpraise, however well meant, is unintentionally

bigoted, the result of white overcompensation and guilt. If a black playwright—*any* playwright—submits work as a professional, he has the need and *right* to be judged as a professional and by professional standards. He must be allowed to be an artist and be judged as an artist, not as a black artist.

*

Obviously, this holds just as true for actors. Racially intimidated directors have been allowing black actors lapses in craft that they would never tolerate in white actors. This creates resentment among white actors, strengthens bad habits in black ones and reinforces racial predispositions in audiences. Fine actors like James Earl Jones, Clarence Williams III, Cleavon Little and Al Freeman, Jr. had to climb the walls of our theater's bigotry to get work, but it is their talent and technique that deserve admiration, not their color. That talent and technique are insulted if the actors are praised as *black* actors, if they are always cast as black characters, or if other actors are unjustly praised, as they are today, just because they are black.

Hundreds of years of oppression, in and out of the theater, cannot be used as an excuse to overlook lapses in craft. This only extends the oppression. Just as the same opportunities must be offered a black actor as a white actor, so the same ability must be demanded of him. Another example of this intimidation syndrome is the usage of black critics for black plays, which may be the ultimate absurdity in racial obeisance.

A black actor should be able to play not only a racially anonymous character but also a white character (yes, in white face—there is such a thing as make-up). This is acting. It is foolish for an actor to be implausibly black in a white role—for example, Diana Sands in "The Owl and

the Pussycat"—just for the sake of some liberal notion ex-
trinsic to the play. A black actor must simply be *an actor*.
He must not be restricted to playing black people in black
plays by black playwrights about black problems. He must
not be made to feel guilty about pursuing a general career
as an actor. After all, isn't that what the whole thing is
about?

The argument that you have to be black to write about
black people is also nonsense. Does anyone restrict black
playwrights from writing about *white* people? There are
white characters in Douglas Ward's "Brotherhood" and
Bullins's "The Pig Pen." Shakespeare wrote about kings
without ever having been one himself. What is art if
not imagination and insight? "The Great White Hope"
was written by the white Howard Sackler and was as per-
ceptive about black people, history and problems as any
play I've yet seen.

*

The theater cannot let artistic policy be dictated by pressure groups. Last year's cancellation by the Yale Repertory
Theater of Sam Shepard's "Operation Sidewinder" because of pressure from black students was unjustifiable,
outrageous and ridiculous. (Then, when the play was done
at Lincoln Center, *Indians* complained.)

White audiences and critics must learn to watch a play
about black people without race consciousness in their
throats; without judging as if they were judging all black
people or, indeed, themselves and their liberalism.

Racism destroys art as it destroys everything it touches,
and double artistic standards are racist. Honest and consistent artistic standards must be maintained or the theater
will be torn from its mooring in esthetics and set afloat
on the unpredictable seas of racial confusion.

Black critic Clayton Riley will reply to Mr. Gottfried next Sunday.

We Will Not Be 'a New Form of White Art in Blackface'

BY CLAYTON RILEY

Look here. Talk to me about the Theater, talk *with* me about it, and I'll tell you of some not so secret wishes. Wishes from the Blackest part of me.

For instance, my recent dreams. Where I perceive the destruction of America through the crumbling fall of the nation's cherished institutions. Let them sink, retire into ash and rubble. Without flame or other obvious assistance. Permit subtlety, let it be cool. A simple destruction, actually, carried forth by deliberate means, seemingly polite efforts piloted, perhaps, by grinning, dependable, and trustworthy former fieldhands, niggers gone crazy with the loss of faith and their own primitive inclinations.

The Theater, for example. In that parochial outpost where the lies of the regime become a sacred trust (despite all claims to the contrary). Begin there.

Start with an assault on the cathedral of make-believe that responsible citizens hold so dear, the place where such men as critic Martin Gottfried and his friends go to pray for the return of the 19th century. (Break it all up, take it apart—ancient stone by ancient stone.)

I mention Gottfried first (though certainly not to the exclusion of others who share the narrow view he outlined recently in these pages) because he seems to want the designation as primary witness for the dying state's defense. Seems to feel his Theater, the concept and design of which was born and still resides in a yesterday of useless and outmoded disciplines, needs to be protected from usurpation by Blacks whose craft and competence are, to his mind, substandard.

*

In one regard, I would agree with him. Blacks in the Theater—and elsewhere—are *not* functioning on the same wavelengths of quality that are acceptable to most white people. It is Gottfried's opinion that they should be. He blandly asserts that in the contemporary theater, "professional and artistic standards are being compromised for the sake of black plays, playwrights and actors; standards of writing, production, performance and judgment are being lowered for blacks."

Well, I've been attending theater in New York for 18 years, six of them as a reviewer seated, frequently, a few shoulders removed from Gottfried. What standards? Is he seeing something I'm not? He is seeing a theater comprised primarily of musical fantasies, inane, stupefying comedies and what tries to pass for profound dramatic commentary on our times. You know, *quality* stuff. By professional standards I suppose he means the sort offered to the public in the work of Neil Simon, he being America's most successful working playwright and a purveyor of comic fare designed to humor us with the helplessness, the impotence and ugliness of characters whose masochistic obsessions America delights in observing.

If "lowering" these standards is what Blacks in the theater are all about, a universal commendation is in order, not the presumptuous assessments offered by Gottfried.

I, too, have criticized the work of Black artists in the theater, most recently those who are with the Negro Ensemble Company. My comments have been severely negative in regard to a repertory theater group Gottfried claims is in existence only because of "the American racial mess," and whose "justification" for being here "is its blackness, not its theater."

Now check that out. I mean, just dig on that for a moment. In a city where there is not a truly impressive white company at work in the performing arts (and I include the self-indulgent Open Theater of Joseph Chaikin), the Negro Ensemble Company needs to justify its existence in terms of some vague, indeed nonexistent framework of excellence that Gottfried has dreamed up and applied to Black theater without mentioning anyone operating in whiteface in the same general arena. If the NEC is a mediocre outfit that mediocrity is basically attributable to an attempt by its director to run his shop as a dictator, and his further attempt to live up to the artistic requirements of white people (and some Blacks, as well) who have been dieting for years on such constipating fare as "Forty Carats" and "Last of the Red Hot Lovers." If NEC concerned itself more with an honest depiction of Black life—which would seriously traumatize both the foundation upon whose financial support the company is slavishly dependent as well as the majority of New York's theatergoing regulars—they would probably accomplish a glorious final season. That, I suggest, is exactly what should happen. NEC's most significant gesture would come in the presentation of one proud work offered on its feet, rather than a hundred plays produced in a kneeling position before its dubious benefactors and the critics.

Nothing in Gottfried's article reveals more about him and the public he serves than these statements: "They [Black playwrights] feel compelled to write about black people and the racial situation" and "The only new black play I've seen that is involved with young, modern, intelligent black men . . . is [Ed] Bullins's "The Pig Pen."

First of all Gottfried sees very few Black plays if he sees

only those presented outside the Black community. Apparently he feels obliged to look only at those works presented on turf that is comfortable and familiar to him. Such a background hardly suits him to the task of directing remarks to anyone about the quality and nature of dramatic presentations drawn from the Black experience. This is an experience that is, on evidence offered by him, totally foreign to all the things he regards as important. Shouldn't he be equally concerned with the fact that virtually every white playwright reveals a compelling desire to write about white people and nonracial situations? And, giving him every benefit of the doubt, can I really assume that what he regularly watches from his aisle seat these evenings is always, or even infrequently, involved with young, modern, intelligent white men? Furthermore, about his contention that "A black actor should be able to play not only a racially anonymous character but also a white character (yes, in white face—there is such a thing as make-up)," I would like to know just which part of our society is now, or has ever been, blessed with such an absurd type of anonymity.

Blacks have existed in this country as Blacks ever since those pirates, pimps, whores and murderers dropped them off at Jamestown in 1619, by way of spreading the gospel of white missionary benevolence to the New World. As Blacks, we have a rich, albeit anguished legacy to call upon when we choose—onstage or anywhere else—to tell one another about ourselves. Those who willingly chose to ignore what we were about until recently are hardly the ones to tell us what forms our craft and our artistic concerns should take, particularly since their silence and indifference were fundamental contributors to the exclusion of Blacks from America's cultural marketplace for so long.

One of the results of that deliberate and carefully

protected history of white-only-with-token-regard-for-the-natives brand of theater is today's reality of dual activity by America's Black actors and playwrights. On the one one hand, there is a theater of Negro participation, in which Blacks work essentially as guests subject to the whims (sometimes known as "standards") of those whites who extend the invitations and control the output. Second, there is the Black Theater, in existence now since the early 1960's. Here we have the locale for all who are removed—to the extent that is possible in this country—from the shackling influences of those who would impose, in the words of Black playwright Ed Bullins, "a new form of white art in blackface."

Most of the work Bullins does is presented in Harlem, or in other Blood-of-the-realm communities. He is, when working "at home," a writer of extraordinary power and insight, whose one exhibited fault is a disappointing lack of range. Yet the depth to which this remarkably talented craftsman has gone in exploring the form and the substance of Blackness as Blacks in America know it, is more than a compensatory factor. Bullins's "Goin' a Buffalo" stands, in my opinion, with LeRoi Jones's "Dutchman" as an example of the most brilliant playwriting ever done in America.

As opposed to the current Broadway musical, "Purlie," which is an example of Negro participation theater at its absolute best, the productions at Ernie McClintock's Afro-American Speech and Drama Studio, 15 West 126th Street, are performed with an eye toward candid and distinct appeal to Black audiences. Whites are as welcome there as they are anywhere else in Harlem, and the style and level of theater speak clearly of a concern for creating and maintaining a body of Black Theater classics. That they can offer a theatrically complete rendering of James Baldwin's "The Amen Corner," followed by sharp, ener-

getic productions of Bullins's "Clara's Ole Man" and
Marvin X's "Taking Care of Business" is a tribute to the
company's versatility and its competence, as well.

Also at work in Harlem is the National Black Theater,
which is into the examination of ritual presentation
through the use of dance and music structured to detail
both the African and African-American tradition of the
shared experience.

*

Roger Furman's New Heritage Theater has struggled
through several financial crises, but manages to hold forth
with solid, informative and entertaining productions of
well-written, imaginatively produced original dramas and
comedies.

None of the companies I have mentioned are beyond
criticism; some of their works (and the works of similar,
community-based theaters) are better than others, and
some of their playwrights, actors and directors are better
equipped than others. This must all be measured by yard-
sticks of performance realistic to the artists and the community involved. But there is magic in what they do. Black
magic for those who know the forms or are willing to sit
and feel the effect without reaching to the shores and caves
of Europe for guidance.

The Black Theater is not Lincoln Center, that gleaming
fortress of second rateness that stands in full-dress tribute
to this nation's deathless commitment to plasticism and
battered sensibilities. And the Black Theater is not Broadway—the safe haven of quick buck ideologists, comman-
ders-in-chief of the nation's lost and drifting spirit, who
direct the collective sense of what is still stubbornly referred to as taste.

Possibly the people working in the Black Theater are no
longer really Americans. Their isolation (may it last, let it

grow) is right now their salvation from the dry-rot of America's banditry and killer ethic, from its shriveled soul and lack of style. Black Theater, if it can hold out long enough against the temptations of Uncle Sam the gold baron, may be able to do its part in symbolically murdering the beast lurking beneath this country's expanding hard hat.

Let latter-day glaciers cover old "standards" in the United States. We don't need them any more than do the people we slaughter in Southeast Asia, in Africa and all other points east in the Third World—the people we put in the ground because they don't find pizza and Cokes a mouth-watering treat, because they don't want to stand in line for a look at the "professional and artistic standards" on sale at "Coco" and "Promises, Promises."

Let the Blacks do it. Let the Blacks display deplorable behavior in all theater lobbies, let them do vulgar, nitty-gritty nasty dancing at the Vivian Beaumont, fill the orchestra pit at the Ambassador, home of "The Boy Friend," with stale bones from a thousand fried chicken legs. Let it be. Let it be now that the old regime tumbles, crushing beneath its ill-gotten fat all "normality," all "courtesy," all wrong versions of what is right.

America deserves the loss of precious, thin-skinned assumptions of what constitutes art and culture. Deserves molasses on the soft cushion of its national theater seat, and a continuing flood of profane invective from every proscenium lip in the land.

Martin Gottfried needs to tell us about standards, like Lester Maddox needs to tell us about good government. Like the Ohio National Guard needs to tell us about the Ten Commandments or the Golden Rule.

If a guideline is needed, we can turn to the music of Black America. Les McCann, a Black man, an artist, a musician, impresses upon me what happens when we try

to live up to what white America has composed as the
"right" melodies, the "correct" lyrics. Black America
strives, McCann suggests, strives to make sense out of life
in a country that has never made genuine sense out of anything.

"Trying' ta make it real," laments McCann in his album
called "Swiss Movement."

"Tryin' ta make it real," he says, speaking of everything
we do and say and feel.

"Tryin' ta make it real," McCann concludes, "compared to what?" Black art will ultimately have to structure
its own forms and a usable value system. Duplicating the
exhausted, death-wish energies, the contradictions and
shattered criteria of the American theater—an "art form"
now populated in exorbitant numbers with its own naked
and sagging bodies and an equally flabby collective consciousness—brings the Black artist into a trap that all people of good will and good sense, Black and White, should
seek to avoid.

Gottfried's Head Start in Drama Criticism

BY JOSEPH OKPAKU

(as unpublished by the New York Times)

After reading Martin Gottfried's article "Is all Black
Theatre Beautiful? No.", I am at a loss whether to be
amused or angry. Mr. Gottfried commits so many errors
of logic, false assertions, erroneous assumptions, critical
ineptitude and an absolute ignorance of the fundamentals
of dramatic creativity that such an article would have
been ignored in a high school magazine in some little vil-
lage in mid-western middle America.

But it is presented in The New York Times, and in particular, in the supposedly elitist *Art and Leisure* section of the Sunday paper. One would like to believe that the reasons for writing and publishing an article would include its insight, its contribution to knowledge, its potential positive influence on the subject it deals with and the skill and professionalism of the writing. It is clear, however, that Mr. Gottfried used the front page of the section to propagandize on his obviously personal resentment of a black presence in what used to be a lily white American theatre. One suspects, in fact, that there are many more white people in the theatre—actors, playwrights, directors and critics—who share Gottfried's selfish narrow-mindedness, and seek to hide their professional incompetence and corresponding lack of success on some scapegoat rationalization such as "the black man has taken over".

First, the false assertions of the article. Gottfried's entire article is based on the assertion that blacks have taken over the American theatre. This assertion has no basis in fact. Although a few black playwrights have had a chance to be produced in the past two years, the opportunity offered playwrights is still so overwhelmingly less than their talent would justify, that any honest person with access to facts would have to conclude that the theatre is still relatively closed to blacks.

Gottfried also claims that standards have been lowered for blacks. This, of course, is false. It is still more difficult for a black playwright or actor of a given talent to be given the same chance his white counterpart has. Gottfried must know this because after all his wild generalities, there are only two theatres, the Negro Ensemble Company and the American Place Theatre, which he gives as examples of those making overtures to blacks. What he does not say is that there are over fifty other theatres in New York.

It seems to me quite clear, in fact, what Gottfried's

problem is. He and a whole bunch of other incompetent white people in the theatre, frustrated by their inability to win acclaim for achievements they are incapable of, cannot understand the fact that a black person could be successful where they are not. It is the old story of the worst white is better than the best black.

Contrary to Gottfried's intentionally falsified assertions, there are some facts about the black man in the American theatre today. One, the quality of white playwrighting to-day is so low that it essentially does not exist. If Gottfried cannot take this painful fact from a black critic, let him refer to Walter Kerr's comment on the subject last fall. The reasons for the poor quality of white American play-wrighting are numerous and understandable. With a growing anti-intellectualism and anti-professionalism in America, came the self-defeating anti-quality and anti-talent. Simultaneously, the commercialism of the gim-mick, making it possible to succeed financially with trivia, encouraged the development of the non-talent. Psycholog-ically, it was the old adage of "anyone can be anything" reaching a premature demise in "anything goes." While this may have succeeded on Wall Street, it was doomed to failure in the arts, simply because the basis of art is talent and professionalism both of which are unique, not ordinary. If one had more space, one could examine the role this social attitude has had on the general low quality of the arts in America.

Furthermore, contrary to Gottfried's quite embarrassing ignorance, social issues and motivations are the very soul of dramatic creativity. Any student of the history of drama should have been taught that in his freshman year in col-lege. It is a known fact that all societies are at their most creative, dramatically, in the period of social, political and philosophical controversy. It is this lack of a cause for white playwrights that is particularly responsible for the obvious shallowness and simple mindedness of most of their plays.

On the other hand, involvement of black minds in socio-political and philoso-ideological controversy has been a great source of creative energy for the black American.

Another reason for the high quality of a handful of black American playwrights and actors is the simple fact that, in addition to talent, these men have been practising their craft for years, and are very highly trained. If Douglas Ward is a successful playwright, it is because, like Arthur Miller, Ward knows every twist and turn of his craft. He has practised playwriting long before many of the "quickie" white playwrights entered high school. It is, therefore, only to be expected that he would be superior to them.

When Gottfried asserts that there is some high quality white American drama that is being lowered for black people, one finds it difficult to believe that he has not been sleeping through the white American plays he has seen. (This is not to criticize him for doing so as most of the plays are boring.) Gottfried is the first person outside of Muscatine, Iowa, to make such a false claim. It is a fact so common that it is taught in schools, that white American theatre, except for a handful of European influenced writers and three or four others, is generally inferior. I am sure black readers would be grateful to Gottfried if he can list five good American plays and playwrights from the past four years.

Gottfried does not seem to realize the obvious fact that white playwrights also recognize the validity of a social motivation. Their pre-occupation with themes of sexual hang-ups and alienation is obviously socially motivated. The only reason that the white playwright has not contributed much to the history of drama with his sexual material is because, as a product of puritan sexual perversion, he is incapable of offering any substantial insight into an area of life which is far more profound than he realizes. Thus he thinks that there is some substantial drama in showing a naked woman on stage. He cannot understand that some women, like men, (in anticipation of Women's Lib), are better clothed since their substantial ugliness should not be exposed to insult the eye. In STUMP, one of the few truly meaningful white dramas of the last season, the low point came when the leading girl, after holding the spectators at a high level of emotional and aesthetic empathy, suddenly took off her clothes as if to remind us that it was white American drama all over again—a fact the spectators had gladly forgotten for an enjoyable hour.

Gottfried also says that there is no place on Broadway for an all black cast. In other words, ethnic consciousness is anti-quality. What he does not say is the fact that the New York theatre is substantially Jewish, a fact Gottfried could not but be familiar with. And it is not anti-semitic to say so. It is for this reason that I have preferred not to call Gottfried a racist or any other names that only confuse the issues, and replace honest debate with polemical hysteria.

Which brings me to perhaps the most disturbing falsehood in the article. Martin Gottfried says, "the argument that you have to be black to write about black people is also nonsense. Does anyone restrict black playwrights from writing about white people?" Such arrant nonsense! First, did Gottfried read the editor's note at the bottom of his article. "Black critic Clayton Riley will reply to Mr. Gottfried?" Second, let Gottfried ask his white editors to provide in this page how many black critics they have asked to review white plays. Also how many black critics who have asked to do so have been turned down. Nor can Gottfried pretend not to know how plays get reviewed.

Will it be pushing the point too strongly to remind Gott-fried that there isn't one black editor in all of *The New York Times*. The truth is that, given the relatively greater maturity of black people, borne of having to cope with life—a crucial prerequisite for criticism—no editor or producer is willing to let a black critic lay his hands on their high budget successful exercise in trivia.

All of the above has been said about a basically stupid article because of the more important issue of a fairer and more meaningful dialogue on dramatic criticism in New York. One would not feel the need to talk about black critics and white critics if black critics have the same op-portunity to judge and influence the performance of the criticism of New York drama that the white critics have. It is not sufficient, in fact it is insulting, to have white critics review all plays, black and white, and then as a token overture, allow black critics do a "second column" review of a black play. Even in this unsatisfactory state, there is, possibly inadvertently, a selection of polemical and inarticulate responses to highly prejudiced and mis-leading articles on black plays. Thus Gottfried writes an unintelligent article. And an unimpressed reader is promised, with a note at the bottom, that there will be a black rebuttal the following Sunday. And then Clayton Riley "does his own selfindulgent thing" in response to an article that could be clearly, simply and articulately de-stroyed without having to talk about American racism or the destruction of American society. This is a great dis-service on the part of the editor to black scholarship and black criticism.

Finally, one cannot help but be disturbed or amused by the most glaring contradiction in the publication of Gott-fried's article. We are made to believe that in order to write for the *New York Times*, one must be able to think, to write, to document assertions, to develop one's arguments, to organize one's thought and to have something substantial to contribute. Gottfried's article is annoying without being provocative, trivial without being interesting, biased without being substantial and above all, very very poorly written.

The question then is: Why did the *New York Times* lower its standards for Gottfried? I cannot help quoting Gottfried. "If this can be defended as a sort of Headstart project, a/does a Headstart project belong in the form of art? b/isn't it condescending? c/do lowered standards encourage or restrict (critical) development?" of such men as Gottfried?

*

Objectivity matters most with the media. Views about blacks filter through a hierarchy of editors, reviewers and critics who delete whatever does not quite conform to their view of themselves in relation to blacks. Substantial elimination of bias will result from the hiring of black editors, not just reporters; from assigning reviews of *white* as well as black artistic works to black critics; by giving by-line coverage of controversial events, racial and otherwise, to black journalists. The point here is that although whites may have cornered the bourbon, hula-hoop and chewing gum markets, they are a long way from tying up objectivity. The solution is simple: prime and equal time for blacks.

Liberalism #5: "There's an opening for a black"

There is an old saying among southern blacks that white is right; meaning that no matter how virtuous, intelligent, hardworking or experienced a given black may be, any "settling" of differences with whites would turn on color.

Power disparities meant that the white man prevailed and the black man kept in his "place". Something of the same understanding is also behind the old white saying, "free, white and twenty-one". Vistas were unlimited for the colorless majority, while for blacks there were only specific, narrow slots.

Liberals are not so unsophisticated as to suggest that blacks should have only maids' and porters' jobs, but there is a subtle notion that certain jobs are appropriate. The converse of this looms large: innumerable jobs are in some vague way considered off-limits for those who are bound, black, and over twenty-one.

It is easy to catalogue the new black positions. They are non-profit, unrelated to the manufacturing of goods, usually non-essential to the economy, dependent upon government funds, foundation support or the whims of the Internal Revenue Service. All such positions could in one broad gesture be eliminated with no dislocation whatsoever to the American economy. Perhaps missed, perhaps mourned, but quickly forgotten. (Who was it who said that the average mourning period for *anything* was no more than six weeks?)

This is not to depreciate the importance of these positions or to suggest that blacks would want to see them eliminated, but a spade is still a spade. Many of these highly visible slots were created under pressure and intended mainly to showcase the university or corporation as an equal opportunity employer. The key distinction about all these occupations is their relative powerlessness and their irrelevance to the body politic. In the universities, blacks are deans of minority affairs or in Black Studies departments. In business, they are personnel officers for special markets, urban affairs specialists, special assistants (or Deputies) to whomever, or vice-presidents in charge of guess who. Black Studies could pass away with only the slightest tremor in the university at large; and the bevy of black corporate urban-affairs specialists could become the victims of an economy move today, never having acquired the technical experience for independent ventures.

For a black, there is a familiar professional cycle: he may start with something civil rightsy, perhaps move over to government for a brief disillusioning stint, try teaching for a while and wind up without the options of the white public-interest careerist.

Whites who have worked in civil rights, armed with good liberal credentials, move on to important and quite different new jobs, like college presidencies. Relatively few blacks, however, have been able to "cash in" on their civil rights stints. The assumption seems to be that because whites entered civil rights out of choice rather than necessity, it was somehow "big" of them and they should now be appropriately rewarded. Thus when whites are civil rights consultants, they are well-paid.

Though civil rights is alleged to be that special bastion of black expertise, the most powerful positions have been reserved for whites. The wealthiest civil rights organization is headed by a white who earns $65,000 a year. The country's best known black civil rights leader, with comparable tenure, earns half that salary. Here again, the keepers of the purse must feel that since a white can be anything in this society, if he chooses a civil rights career, he should be rewarded at the level of the job opportunities he has "sacrificed". Blacks do not overlook that private white contributions diminish when blacks take the helm.

BLACK BUSINESS

Many whites, and some blacks too, show surprise upon learning that a particular black business venture is succeeding. If it is competing with white businesses, the incredulity can cause total misperception. A young black woman's experience with an old college friend is typical. The two former classmates had not seen each other for several years and decided to bring each other up to date over brunch one bright Saturday morning. The black woman told her old school chum about her husband's efforts to start a publishing house; she briefly described the company's first titles, most of which dealt with subjects of national concern, albeit non-racial. Some months later, a white mutual friend of the two women met the black woman at a reception. Their conversation:

"I understand from Esther that you're married now. Congratulations."

"Thank you," the woman replied.

"She mentioned that your husband is a publisher . . ."

"Right."

". . . and that he's going to be publishing mainly . . ." The young man groped for words.

". . . mainly ghetto books."

"I told Esther *books*, just books."

Which of the two whites dreamed up the "ghetto books" is not important. (What are such books?—of, by and for the ghetto, perhaps?) The "mistake" reveals the common difficulty in adjusting to the idea that black entrepreneurs may provide goods and services for *everyone*, not only black people.

In many aspects, whites are a natural market for the productive energies of black businessmen. Survival has dictated

that blacks become experts on whites, on their tempera-
ments, approaches to life, child-rearing customs, spending
habits, ego needs and mating practices. And besides, whites
still have more money than blacks. It doesn't take an Adam
Smith to choose between a dime and a diamond.

With such expertise why is it that black capitalism
hasn't touched white markets? Despite grandiose claims
which conjure up images of gleaming black manufacturing
and banking enterprises, the truth is that most organizations established to spur black business mainly support
fried chicken franchises, nickle and dime stores, service businesses like cleaners, barber shops, beauty salons—and then,
only if they intend to locate in black neighborhoods.
(Some nationalists encourage the confinement of black
businesses to their areas and oppose the concept of "non-
racial" black enterprises out of the mistaken belief that the
proliferation of such small ventures will eventually render
these communities independent of the rest of America.)

On "Keeping Them in Their Place"

Efforts to confine blacks to particular slots and issues has a
self-fulfilling effect. It encourages reality-oriented young
blacks to commit their lives to the solution of the race
problem; it reinforces the general impression that blacks
can address themselves effectively to racial matters only.
Even among blacks, there is the notion that one choosing
to pursue some non-racial occupation or to speak publicly
about an essentially non-racial issue has somehow aban-
doned his people. There is the feeling that too much
remains racially undone for blacks to have the luxury of
time-consuming artistic, scientific or intellectual concerns.

When blacks attempt to extricate themselves from occupational cubby holes, the stereotyped thinking of even the best-intentioned whites becomes manifest. Recall the presumptuousness that many read into Martin Luther King's daring to speak out on such a "complicated political matter" as the war in Vietnam. He should stick to race, many said; what does he know about international politics, still others asked; and some who regarded themselves as civil rights supporters argued that he would lose adherents to the black cause by identifying with the anti-war movement, ignoring King's insistence that the black struggle and the anti-war effort were closely related. For whites, however, there was no similar contradiction when Benjamin Spock, the baby doctor, became a leading anti-war spokesman, or when the Berrigans, two Catholic priests, issued manifestos on the immorality of war, or when Ralph Nader, a lawyer from nowhere, emerged and took on the colossus, General Motors. What criticism there was of Spock was aimed at his lending his enormous prestige to the then radical, anti-war protest and not at his moving into a new area of non-expertise.

How to Break the Cycle

People can do what they're given a chance to do. Usually. This is the heart of the American creed.

Breaking the cycle that cubbyholes blacks begins with making the mind a blank screen about what are "appropriate" black activities. It also means that liberals must cease and desist from accusing blacks who seek mainstream jobs of deserting their people. This is a decision for blacks to make, not whites.

Although whites have been running this country since its bloody and violent inception, the spate of problems with public schools, unemployment, pollution, housing, health, peace, and sex shows that there's ample room for improvement. An influx of blacks into heretofore off-limit areas might indeed be the fresh stimulus a tired and frustrated nation needs. Things could hardly get any worse.

Liberalism #6: "It's not because you're black"

The response is almost Pavlovian. A black describes some especially awful treatment. His white friend can match the incident: "Something like that happened to me, too. It's not because you're black!!" But many a black has understood that the situations were not truly parallel. Simply because whites, too, experience insults, abuses, injustices, or humiliations does not mean that their misfortunes have identical causes. Medgar Evers was shot for one reason, and Bobby Kennedy for another. The latter's assassination does not make the former's any less racial.

Whites charge that blacks are paranoid about the prevalence of racial slights. They may be correct—about a *tiny* fraction of the insensitive, rude or offensive behavior aimed at blacks. The problem with the white opinion is that it hardly comes from neutral bystanders to the American racial drama.

Until the disparities of black life, as seen in housing, jobs and education are eliminated, that infinitesimal number of instances when there was no racial offense is irrelevant.

The moment the black American feels at home in his country he'll hear a white say, "It's not because you're black"—and believe it.

Living Up to Liberalisms:
Portraits of Blacks Who Tried

Liberalisms, like the labels for blacks, have shifted with black protests and progress. These frequent shifts have prompted some intricate footwork by those blacks who assumed that by living up to liberal expectations, "success" would be theirs.

Not too long ago, living up to liberalisms took the form of attempting to refute specific white criticisms of blacks, which at that stage focused on cleanliness, morality, education, and proper deportment.

The "black who tried" worked hard for his education; then they told him he was "overqualified" for the clerk-type jobs, those visible white-collar ones that required little skill but provided a steady, reliable income. With those jobs for which he was truly qualified, he met a regretful, "It isn't me, I would hire you. It's the others."

The same refrain followed him into white neighborhoods (where the better housing was). The polite refusals of prospective sellers implicated neighbors as being the ones who would resent the sale. "Of course, you'll understand."

If he finally found a neighborhood, he tried his darndest to keep the lawn and shrubbery up so that falling property values would never be blamed on him. To his sometimes unrecoverable amazement, he saw all the neighbors, who daily complimented him because he and his children were "different", one by one moving out.

He normally ended up in some civil service work but still clung to the conviction that a little more effort was all that was needed, and he counseled his children in the ways of proving to whites that they were different from other blacks.

His generation of blacks had faith that whites were serious when they said that all they wanted was for blacks to be civilized. He was certain that hard work, thrift, cleanliness, concern for property, education and summer camps for the kids would eliminate the stigma of color.

He was wrong.

Meanwhile, he passed on to his children the mission of living up to liberalisms. Whereas he had gone to a southern college——and that might have been one of the reasons he wasn't "accepted"——his children would go to white universities. Their "ings" and "eds" would flow naturally, diction being insisted upon along with table manners, neat dress, conservative colors (if any) and, of course, deodorant.

He was never quite sure whether he had mastered all the essentially white attributes, but there would be no question about his children.

They carried the banner admirably. They made white friends and brought them home——at last. They integrated Boy Scout troops and camps. It was important, of course, that everyone remember that socializing stop short of romance, but that did not rule out interracial doubledating.

The children became doctors, dentists, teachers, and caseworkers——independent or safe governmental positions and professions. They avoided those situations which would give the lie to their cherished belief that as "exceptions" to prevailing black types, they were practically white.

Those with stronger convictions about their "special-

ness" carried their fantasies to white law firms, corporations, businesses, and universities——only to find polite
promises to "keep in touch" should a position "open".
Many of them then wandered into racial-type positions—
—the Urban League, NAACP, or their counterparts. It was
the beginning of a civil-rights mentality, with liberals as
friends.

It was the era of "blacks and whites together" and "We
Shall Overcome". But in strategy sessions and planning
meetings, the little signs of dominance cropped up. Familiarity bred familiarity. When bail-money was needed,
whites could get it. The shedding of *their* blood brought
public outrage. When *they* grew weary, publishers' offers,
consulting contracts, foundation grants, and think-tank invitations awaited them.

The week-end warriors and TV cameras gone, our black
——still trying——saw the true proportions of the problems for the first time.

When he first spoke of power for *his* people——political
office, money, business, manufacturing, finance——his
white friends accused him of separatism. Others who were
not friends called it reverse racism. He puzzled over the dis-
crepancy between what they had and what he wanted. All
right. He would go it alone. He gave up on liberalisms. Living up to anything they said was irrelevant.

6

What Next?

By now, we hope enough has been said.

Change comes hard. It means shedding old ways which are often preferred whether they work or not. At least they're familiar.

But the white reader who has read these pages and reached this point has at least one thing in his favor. Motivation. And that makes changing a little easier.

Repetition also helps. Readers who still perceive that polite freeze from a black they've really been trying to get to know might consider a second, a third, or perhaps even a fourth reading. It's worth the effort.

Nationally, blood pressures will go down and ulcers heal —some of them, at least—from whites seriously trying to get along with black folks.

ABOUT THE AUTHORS

SHEILA RUSH, now Sheila Okpaku, is a graduate of Chatham College and Harvard Law School. A Trustee of Chatham College and former Director of the Communitt Law Offices in New York City, Mrs. Okpaku is an Associate Professor of Law at Hofstra Law School.

CHRIS CLARK, a former dean at Bryn Mawr College, where she had her undergraduate education, is a graduate of Yale Law School. She is presently an attorney for CBS.

Sheila Rush Okpaku

Chris Clark